# SILENT SCARS

The True Story of Linda Gilman

I0438838

By

Linda Gilman and Jarod Gilman

with Mary Ann Renlon, Ph.D.

© Copyright 1994, Gilman

ISBN: 1-58500-162-7

Linda Gilman is a survivor. We all experience tests of our physical and mental strength, but Linda's unique series of traumas haunted her until they drove her to the brink of insanity. For four long months, Linda would face horrors of her dysfunctional childhood family while coming to terms with an unexpected and unwanted psychic gift that frightened her. "Why me?" she often thought. What is so special about Linda Gilman?

Silent Scars is the true story of Linda Gilman's personal and psychic transformation. Through a divine intervention, Linda experienced major psychic dreams that warned her of impending disasters (including the death of her father one week before it happened), a breakdown or breakthrough over her unresolved childhood pain, a memory from another lifetime that played out in this lifetime, forgiveness of a dead parent and a clairsentient ability to use words that are well beyond her comprehension to help her to understand someone's emotional state. Before she was to break through her pain and fears, Linda also had a near death experience where, although she is Jewish and did not believe in Jesus as our savior, she left her body and he came and spoke to her.

Today, Linda has found new levels of happiness as she has learned to accept her psychic gift and incorporate it into her life. Linda spent several years writing her book, "Silent Scars", because she believes her story should be shared.

- Linda Gilman

This book is dedicated to my parents,
Ruth and Ellis.

## Acknowledgments

I am happier and more at peace with myself than I have ever been. Special thanks to the following people for the support and love they have shown me throughout my illness and the process of writing this book.

First and foremost, I would like to thank my family: my saintly husband, Chuck Gilman; my two dynamic sons, Jarod and Michael; and my strongest advocate, my mother, Ruth.

I would also like to thank my dear friends for all of their support and encouragement: Carol Goldenberg; Pam and Lew Bornstein; Janet Sclaroff; Sharon Schwartz; and a special thanks to my wonderful editor, Julie Seltzer.

Jarod thanks his parents for entrusting him with this project as well as providing constant encouragement and love. Jarod would also like to thank all the people who made his life a little brighter as he struggled with this monumental task.

# Foreword

**catharsis** (ka-'tharh-sis):

1) the act of ridding or cleansing; 2) the relief of the emotions gained through viewing the experiences of others, especially in a drama; 3) the relieving of a neurotic state by re-enacting an earlier emotional experience.

# Chapter 1

I bolted up in bed. The sun was streaming through the blinds. I looked out the window. The pin oaks were beginning to change color. It would be a warm, lazy day in late August of 1988--a day to forget the emotional storms that were chasing me even as I slept. But the force of the dream woke me.

I had dreamt that I was watching TV in the sunken fireplace pit of my living room when all of a sudden my parents opened the door to our home and burst into the room. They yelled, "You've got to help us carry things in from the car!" I didn't want to. I wanted to stay in the peaceful calm of my living room. As my mother stepped forward, I noticed that her hands were tied behind her back. Now it was my turn to yell.

"Why did you tie her up like that?" My father opened his mouth, started to scream at me and, then, dropped flat on his face. He had died of a heart attack.

Quickly I ran to the kitchen, got a knife, and cut the ropes on my mother's hands. I never did bring in the things from the car.

When I went downstairs to tell my husband Chuck about my dream, he listened patiently. Then, he turned back to his tasks. I could tell that he didn't give the dream too much importance. "Chuck, don't take this lightly," I admonished him. "The dream scared me!"

"Look, Honey, you haven't been able to sleep well lately. I'm not too surprised that you had a disturbing dream."

What did I expect? I reminded myself that Chuck is a mathematical genius. His mother told me that he was a child prodigy in math. His family always had everything organized and under control. Of course, his logical mind would not allow him to identify with dreams and what they might mean.

Still, I could not shake the effects of that dream. Why had it come to me? My father was in good health, so what could it mean? Mom and Dad were enjoying their retirement. "It must be my nerves," I thought to myself.

I started my afternoon exercises. When I exercise, I often work out my problems. I was just finishing when I received a phone call from Sandy. Sandy, the director of my eldest son Jarod's youth group, had struck up a friendly relationship with me. She called to tell me when our next youth group meeting would be, and she was about to hang up when I blurted, "Sandy, I had a terrible dream." Without giving her time to reply, I launched into my dream. Sandy, who is a considerate person, treated my story with respect. I concluded by telling her that I just needed to tell somebody.

Sandy said, "Hope to God, it doesn't happen!" This comment raised a new concern.

Although my father and I hadn't spoken for three months, I felt I had to call him. Despite my difficulty in communicating with him, I truly loved him, and I was genuinely worried about him. What if the dream came true? What if he died and I had the guilt of not speaking to him?

I knew his phone number by heart. "Hi, it's Linda. So...how are you doing?" I could tell by the sound of his voice that he was surprised to hear from me.

"Fine. Your mother's not here now."

I couldn't blame him for being abrupt. After all, I usually had only a few words to say to him, a carry-over from my teen years when I had done my very best to avoid him.

"That's okay, Dad. I called to talk to you."

Now he was really surprised. "You're lucky you got me. I just came in from walking Maggie." Maggie was the name he had given to the dog I had found years ago, abandoned and in desperate need of a home. Why my father agreed to take in this mangy-looking mutt, I will never know--but he did.

'How is Maggie--spoiled as ever?"

He chuckled and said, "I'm so glad you found Maggie and brought her to us. We really love her."

"Yes, I know. Is she still sleeping with you and Mom?"

"So where else?"

I was happy to hear the ease in his voice--a quality I had missed during my growing years when he had toiled as a pharmacist from sun up to sun down in our family drug store.

"How's your golf game?" I asked, trying to extend myself beyond my usual, "Hi, Dad, how-are-you-is mother-there" routine.

"Fine. I went out Saturday morning and beat Harry by ten strokes. Was he mad! Harry hates to lose."

"You'd better be careful...maybe he won't go with you next time."

Dad laughed. "He's got no choice. Harry's got no one else. His regular golf partner died last spring." It was a pleasant, unhurried conversation. Dad was using his theatrical voice--the one he used when he played Tevya in Fiddler on the Roof at the Community Center Theater.

Saying goodbye, I felt satisfied. "There, I guess that the dream had me worried for nothing," I assured myself. Dad was fine.

Exactly one week later on August 30, 1988, I received

an urgent phone call from my parents' neighbor who happened to be a nurse. She informed me that my father had suffered a heart attack. She said that she had called an ambulance and that my father had been taken immediately to Our Lady of Lourdes Hospital.

Chuck and I were ready in minutes. We hurried to the car. As we pulled out of the driveway, I turned to Chuck and said, "My father is dead." It was something I instinctively knew. I was glad my husband's sports car was fast because I knew how important it was for us to get to the hospital quickly.

When we arrived, we went straight to the waiting room. My mother looked very strained. My brother Larry was attempting to comfort her, explaining to us that she was on the verge of hysteria. He told me not to ask her too many questions as she was in shock. Larry then told us how my father had died.

Dad had been outside raking leaves. The paper boy knocked at the door and told my mother that there was a man lying on the front lawn. As she stepped outside the house, she found my father lying flat on his face on the lawn. Later, the doctor informed her that my father had died instantly of a massive heart attack. I hoped my seventy-four year old father hadn't suffered much, but since there were no witnesses, I doubted this could ever be confirmed.

I knew I had to see my father. No one had the nerve to see his body now that the doctor had officially pronounced him dead. But I knew I had to see him. I had to tell my father the things I hadn't been able to tell him when he was alive. So, I mustered the courage to ask where his room was. Strangely enough, even as I entered the sterile room, I felt his presence. Then, like the downpour of a summer storm, all of the anger I had held tightly inside me burst forth suddenly. I screamed at him, "Why did you do to me what you did? Why were you so hard on us?"

I stepped closer and looked directly at his lifeless body. I fixed my eyes on his handsome face. Maybe now that he was still, he would have to listen to me. "Why couldn't I ever talk to you?" I challenged him. "Why were our lives filled with violence?" There was no answer. "Didn't you know that I loved you?" Now the tears were falling softly from my eyes. I propped myself against his bed for support. "Didn't you know I wanted a happy family life? Why did this happen?" I knew I could not forgive my father for making my early years so miserable.

On the way home, Chuck tried to calm me. In spite of his best efforts, inside myself I knew no peace. My father's death only served to stir up the murkiness that lay just beneath the surface of my happy existence.

Later that night, I made a round of calls to my friends. When I called Sandy, she said, "Oh, my God, Linda...the dream!" I was amazed and horrified at the same time. I was amazed to realize that my father's death, which seemed so sudden and completely unexpected, was something that I actually had been told before it had happened. But I was horrified, too. Was I supposed to have prevented his death? Is that why I had the dream? Or was my father's death pre-destined?

Next, I dialed my close friend, Carol. I knew she would carefully listen to my story. I also hoped that somehow she would be able to tell me whether or not I had some strange power higher than most humans--a power that enabled me to see future events--or whether the correlation between my dream and my father's death was merely a coincidence.

I let the phone ring and ring. Finally, her answering

machine turned on. As it clicked, I remembered that Carol had gone on a trip with her husband and would not be back for a few more days. I did leave a message informing her of my father's death and asking her to return the call as soon as possible.

I knew I could count on Carol. In some senses, we were mirror twins. If I told her that I had a pain in my right arm, she would simultaneously and unknowingly be having a pain in her left arm. The same day that my husband decided to close his apparel manufacturing company in Manhattan to develop a business to run from home, her husband gave up his home office to form a large sales company. Whenever I felt down, Carol was good for a laugh and vice versa. Although I tend to be a bit of a recluse and love to stay in my house, I am fortunate to have a cherished network of friends I can count on. Carol is one of those friends.

In the days that followed, I began to do a lot more thinking about the dream. Maybe if I examined the dream piece by piece, I could discover exactly what it meant. By now, I figured that the first part of the dream referred to my early years. These were stressful years with many nasty surprises. Were those years about to intrude upon the adult life I had so carefully built?

My younger son Michael, who was in junior high at the time, knew how important the dream was to me. I wanted to confide in him even though I really didn't expect him to understand the dream any better than I did.

My friend Pam thought that the most interesting part of the dream was the part about my mother's hands tied behind her back. But what did it mean? Did it have something to do with the way my father had mistreated her in their marriage? I did not like my mother for being so weak. I desperately wanted her to defend Larry and me when we were young, but she never did. I knew she had been a teacher when she met my father, so she couldn't have been that weak. Why didn't she stand up to my father when he mistreated us--her own children?

I was relieved when Carol got back from her vacation. One afternoon, she called to invite herself over to my house. She said that she loved to walk through my heavily wooded neighborhood. As soon as Carol stepped into the foyer, her warm smile set me at ease. We hugged each other, and as I invited her in, I immediately proceeded to tell her about my dream and my father's subsequent death. I waited for her reaction, hoping she would tell me my dream was special.

She said she was surprised to hear how vivid my dream was. She said it would be interesting to know why I didn't help carry things in from my parents' car. She thought the part about my mother's bound hands symbolized how helpless my father had rendered her throughout the marriage.

Despite her interest in the dream, I could tell that Carol did not believe I had psychic powers. Of course, I really didn't believe it, either. Or maybe I didn't want to believe it. Why would anyone believe that I possessed special powers? I was a housewife and mother. I only went to a junior college, and I never was a great student. Why should Linda Gilman suddenly be a lightning rod for psychic warnings? It just didn't make sense.

When I told Chuck about Carol's visit, he seemed satisfied that one of my friends had seen the logical side of my experience and, basically, sided with him. I ignored his victory. As someone who does not believe in coincidence, I knew the dream had some significance, and I was determined to pursue the meaning of my unusual dream.

Every Sunday, Chuck reads the newspaper. While Chuck buries himself in the business news, I keep the TV listings and circle all of the programs I might like to watch during the week. One program caught my attention immediately. It was a listing for an afternoon talk show. The blurb announced that dream analysts would appear on the program on Tuesday afternoon as special guests. I made sure to circle the date and time on my calendar.

The day of the show, I made certain not to answer any telephone calls so that I could stay glued to the set. One of the experts on the show was lecturing on what he called the "characteristics" of psychic dreams. He explained to the host that a person who experiences a psychic dream, rather than an ordinary dream, bolts up from his/her dream state instead of gradually waking. He said the dream becomes so intense that the sleeper tries to escape by waking up. This made sense to me. Then, he said that the sharpness of the experience or the jolt that the dreamer experiences creates a powerful need to tell the dream to at least two other people. He also added that some people have only one in a lifetime while others have multiple psychic dreams. He warned that only time would tell.

Now I was completely fascinated because he was describing what happened to me! As I listened, I wrote down his ideas so that I could analyze my own dream further. Towards the end of the program, this same expert said that the events which occurred in a psychic dream would unfold in real life within two weeks.

As soon as I turned off the set, I called Pam. I said I was certain my dream qualified as a psychic dream. I certainly had been startled as I bolted up in bed. I also told Pam that, following the dream, I immediately described it to Chuck and Sandy. "Something forced me to tell that dream," I insisted.

Pam did not need to be reminded that my father died less than two weeks after the dream. "He fell on his face just like you saw in the dream." Pam had told her husband Lew about the dream. Lew, who had been a rabbi, said there were explanations for this in the Kabbalah, the book of Jewish mysticism.

"Why is this happening to me?" I asked Pam, not really expecting an answer.

Pam seemed to believe that I would eventually find out why the dream had come to me. Still, I spent the rest of the afternoon wondering, "Why me? Why now? Now, when I have everything a person could want--a loving, successful husband, two sensitive and intelligent children, and a lovely home in a peaceful, wooded area. Why would I want such a message?"

Whatever the reason, I knew that I did not wish to be disturbed. What had happened so many years ago had been tucked away like an unwanted wedding gift in the darkest corner of the attic. I had everything to live for--a pleasant life to look forward to. The brief flattery I felt at the idea that I was the special chosen one to whom the dream revealed itself had been shattered by my rude awakening that somehow my life would never again be the same. I didn't want change. Change was painful!

I escaped to the exercise room. I set up a furious pace on my bike. The unchanging rhythm of the pedaling soothed me and lulled me into thinking that everything would turn out for the better. Whatever this psychic thing was, it would be banished. I would not allow this mystery into my happily content home.

As I continued to pedal, I focused on the far corner of

the room where the ceramic fortune-telling weight scale stood proudly. It appeared the same as when it was an attraction in my father's pharmacy. All these years, it remained accurate to the half pound, which was necessary to detect any slight fluctuation in my weight. I wanted to maintain the 105 pounds on my four foot eleven inch frame. Just as I had done as a child, I would read the fortunes that appeared on the moveable belt at the top of the scale, right below the weight indicator. As my body relaxed into its daily workout, my mind began to sift through the thoughts that were haunting me since my father's death.

Now that my father had died, I didn't know if I wanted to become closer to my mother. She completely relied upon my father all these years, and I knew that she would need to lean on me now that he was gone. I had always prided myself on being the strong one. I would not buy into my father's games. I was my father's favorite, and I would use my favored status to protect my mother and my brother from my father's worst outbursts. Still, I wasn't sure if I was ready to accept the responsibility of my mother's complete dependence.

Looking back on my life, I figured I always did better when I thought of someone else's problems instead of my own. I had often been selfish. And, when I was especially selfish, I often had a pin prick of conscience. I would think of my grandmother who always had something to give to others. Why couldn't I be more like her? Since the dream, I started to re-think some of the things I had done wrong in life. I guess that I was beginning to feel that I had to give back a portion of what I had received.

Maybe these thoughts were entering my mind because my father died so suddenly. One of the things I had always feared as Dad grew older was what I should do with my mother when he eventually died. I knew she would be very emotional--that I could deal with. But I still could not accept her complete and utter dependence upon him. She relied on my father for everything from a ride to the market (since she never learned to drive a car) to basic finances.

Now that he was actually gone, my mother faced organizing a house bursting with the memorabilia of thirty years of family living. My father was a pack rat. Somewhere, carefully preserved in the basement, was the Snow White and the Seven Dwarfs lunch box I had carried with me to school each day. Tucked away in odd corners were dozens of achievement awards and certificates of merit earned by my brilliant brother as well as scores of items not easily identifiable now that my father was not here to catalogue his treasures.

I knew that the only way my mother would be able to get through all of her newfound problems would be by my teaching her to become independent. But the truth was that a side of me had absolutely no desire to help her. Even though I loved her, I was still angry at her for having abandoned me and for having taken my father's side for all those years. I felt as if she didn't deserve my help. She should have thought more of Larry and me instead of my father since we were likely to outlive him. But she didn't, and now she would suffer.

Yet, in the midst of this angry and confused swarm of thoughts, I recalled the dream. In the dream, the first thing I did after my father died was to cut my mother's hands free from the rope. With that in mind, it was no longer a question of whether or not I wanted to help her, but whether or not I should follow the dream. Hadn't the first part of the dream come true? I had always believed in spirit guides, and I had to consider that this dream may have been a message from my spirit guides. Suddenly, I was compelled to help her.

## Chapter 2

Chuck is father, mother, and lover to me. When I first met Chuck, I was seventeen. It was the summer of '64, a cloudless day on the beach in Atlantic City. By the time I met Chuck, I had already developed into one hot teenager with thick, shiny dark brown hair and a shapely petite figure. I wore my hair straight down to my waist. Also, I had a bouncy energy and an attitude that boys found sexy. Boys were always attracted to me. Maybe they liked me because I'm little and they thought I needed protection. Needless to say, dating boys became my favorite activity. I enjoyed the company of boys because they were challenging, interesting, and they gave me lots of attention.

I used to tell my parents that I was going to the library to study. Sometimes I even brought my books with me. I wasn't lying to them, but I wasn't telling them the whole truth, either. I would actually study traits of boys, mainly success traits. I would watch a boy and right away I could tell if he had the characteristics of a winner or not. I knew I wanted a winner, so I dated many boys and got to know different personality types.

After I had gotten to know Chuck, I saw in him all the traits that I wanted in a husband: hard working, goal-oriented, devoted, loving, good-looking, and passionate. We dated for four and a half years, but we also dated others. Before we married, Chuck and I had achieved something quite rare--we had become best friends.

Because my husband and I share so much, I had expected him to be as interested in my dream as I was.

Whenever a friend of mine would ask me about my dream, I would mention that I thought the dream might be psychic. Whenever someone asked Chuck what had really happened, he always threw in the possibility that it was just a coincidence that parts of my dream actually came true. Chuck said that he always knew that I had a sixth sense which let me see things that other people didn't see. In particular, he admired the accuracy of my instincts, especially with regard to other people. Furthermore, Chuck always gave me credit for encouraging him to start Apparel Connections International in 1984.

Starting a new business was a difficult decision for us. It meant that Chuck had to close his prestigious 7th Avenue designer sportswear company. But I could see the increasing number of hours he spent working, and I felt that the kids needed a live-in father. Also, Chuck needed a change.

Sometimes it's harder for me to explain what my husband does in his current business than it is for me to explain my unusual dream. Apparel Connections International is a licensing company. Chuck represents multi-million dollar companies with powerful brand names. These companies become licensors. Chuck uses his connections and negotiating skills to put together deals in which other multi-million dollar companies use those powerful brand names on their products. These companies become licensees. In the course of business, Chuck meets and socializes with many exciting and brilliant presidents and C.E.O.'s of companies.

Although Chuck's business is quite lucrative today, starting the business was scary for us. In the beginning, there are a million things to learn about the particular business. How do you find suitable clients? How do you form agreements which will benefit both the company you represent and the companies who license the products? How are the licensed products marketed? It took courage for Chuck to leave one industry and venture into an unknown one.

But I had confidence in Chuck's ability, and we were rewarded soon after we started. It was 1984, and we had been in business for only a few months. Chuck decided to attend a licensing trade show in New York City to prospect for clients. Chuck does not just visit a show. In his methodical way, he walks up and down each aisle, observing booths which are of potential interest. At this show, he had spent six hours wading up and down the aisles, yet he did not see any companies which caught his eye. He took time out for a pit stop before attacking the final aisle.

As he was returning to the main floor, he climbed some stairs and almost tripped over a four-hundred pound pig who, fortunately, was restrained on a leash by one of the exhibitors. Even the cynical Chuck could not help thinking that this might be an omen. Well, at least it woke him up! As he eased back onto the busy floor, a neon-lit booth caught his eye. The booth was highly stylized and had a fresh look to it as did the energetic, charismatic man behind it. Chuck stopped. His eyes were riveted on the booth. The man at the booth made immediate contact and proceeded to seek out Chuck. The man introduced himself as Robert Greenberg, president of a fledgling but profitable company he artfully called, "L.A. Gear." Chuck told me that the company had sales of five million dollars, but Robert boasted that within five years L.A. Gear would be a half-billion dollar company.

"Linda, do you remember the old days at Al-Mae when

I used to invite you along to business dinners and you would use your incredible intuition to advise me whether or not I should do business with someone?"

I nodded, knowing what he was asking.

"Linda, let me put it this way. I am impressed with Robert Greenberg and with L.A. Gear, but should I spend so much time on a client that I don't know that much about?"

"When are you bringing him to dinner?"

Chuck laughed. "What are you doing Saturday night?"

Since I don't like to cook, the dinners are fun. Though I tend to be shy by nature, I psyche myself up for these dinners. On the one hand, business dinners are an integral part of the business world. Since I chose to marry a man I knew would be successful in business, I expected myself to overcome my shyness in these situations. On the other hand, Chuck wants and needs my talents, and that fact alone helps me to gather my courage. After all, one thing I have confidence in is my intuition.

At the dinner, Robert told me his goals. What impressed me about Robert Greenberg was not only his goals, but how he planned to achieve them. Throughout the dinner, his charm and charisma drew me to him. He had the unmistakable signs of a winner, a confidence I would liken to Johnny Carson. After Robert left, I not only told Chuck that he had made the right decision in taking him on as a client, I told him to devote himself to Robert Greenberg because someday he would make it big. I don't know exactly how I knew it, but I did. I did know that Robert and Chuck shared a similar trait--they were both driven for success.

From 1985 on, L.A. Gear started booming just like Robert said it would. Our company was signing on more and more licensees for L.A. Gear. Then, in 1986, L.A. Gear went public. Now we had a chance to cash in our rewards for a deal Chuck had negotiated in 1984 that injected new life into L.A. Gear. In recognition of the value of that deal as well as a means of providing a continuing incentive, Robert had promised to give us stock options in the future when the company would go public.

The year before my dream, L.A. Gear was putting a lot of pressure on Chuck to give up his own company and join L.A. Gear as an executive. His mission was to be the overseer of the licensing program for L.A. Gear. The catch was that we would have to move to California. At first, the thought of fleeing from the cold New Jersey winters caught our imaginations. But as I meditated on this offer, I knew something was wrong.

When I confronted Chuck about my doubts, his face had a clear look of disappointment.

"Chuck, in your heart you are an entrepreneur. If you join Robert's business, you will lose your independence." Chuck agreed that being his own boss was important to him. "Besides," I continued, "the atmosphere in L.A. is different. So many people in L.A. have second and third marriages. It's a whole different lifestyle. I don't want to lose what we have going for us."

"I can tell you won't be happy there."

"I'm sorry, Chuck."

"Don't be sorry. But I know when I tell Robert that we're turning him down, he won't like it. We may lose some business."

"Better to lose some business than to lose our independence," I insisted.

Chuck kissed me and I knew I had made the right decision. I didn't want to lose business, but we could always develop more. What I really didn't want to lose was Chuck.

***

The timer on my exercise bike beeped, so I stopped my exercising. I really should call my mother. I hadn't heard from her in over a week. When I last called her, she complained about how she had so much to do that she just couldn't get started.

"There's too much to organize," she whined.

While I sympathized with her, I knew she had to do these chores on her own. I helped her break down her tasks into units which she could manage. We continued to talk, and little by little, we made a list of what she should do for the next week. She told me maybe that was what her doctor meant when he advised her to take each day at a time.

Despite my resentment towards my mother for failing to defend my brother and me, I was getting closer to her and beginning to find out more about her. Not having my father to tell her what to do forced my mother to start to make her own decisions. And even though she was still complaining more than actually putting a plan together and working toward a solution, I had to admit that she was making some progress.

My friend Mary Ann in California explained that I was taking over the mother role and that the mother and daughter roles were being reversed. She told me that this was natural as we grew older.

"But I don't want to be her mother!" I protested.

"It's not that you're her mother," she restated. "But you have to do some motherly tasks for her like listening to her stories even if she repeats them and giving her the best advice you can when she needs it from you."

"I guess I can do some of that...but I still feel angry at her." Mary Ann assured me that my anger would not prevent me from helping her and that helping her might actually get rid of some of my anger.

"It's a healing process for both of you," she said earnestly. That's what I liked about Mary Ann. She always made sense even if she sometimes told me things I really didn't want to hear. I guess that's what makes her a good therapist. She listens to me carefully and makes suggestions, but she expects me to do most of the work. One time she told me that the process of working towards finding myself is called, "self-actualization," and it's the highest state of functioning in the real world.

Deep down inside I knew that Mary Ann was right. I promised myself that I would give my mother the best advice I could. I had to stop resenting the fact that she was so weak. Instead, I had to help her to be stronger.

The next day, I talked to my mother for at least an hour. She told me that every time she would start to clean the basement, she would end up crying. She said that even though she knew she had to get rid of the hundreds of boxes and bottles of medicine, cartons of first-aid kits, and even used crutches that he lent to his customers, she still would remember the old days in the store with my father. After listening to her story, I told her that I was going to give her a new name.

"Your name is not Ruth. Your name is actually Ruth-Mildred. Mildred is your weak personality, and Ruth is your strong personality."

"Linda, I might be upset, but I don't have a split personality!" she cried indignantly.

"Mother, that's not what I mean," I explained. "We all

have more than one side to ourselves. You must learn to rely on what Ruth says and not on what Mildred says because Mildred always tries to bring you down."

There was a long pause. Finally, mother responded, "I know you're trying to help me, but I will have to think about Ruth-Mildred." At least she did not reject the idea all together.

I promised to call her again the next day. When I hung up the phone, I felt excited. Even though she did not quite understand all I was trying to tell her, she was listening to me. For the first time in my life, I was being a good daughter to her. I had dropped all the pain so we could become friends.

The following day, we had another long heart-to-heart talk. When I asked her what she had been able to throw out, she said that she actually had thrown out two boxes of pharmaceutical samples. "You're getting there, Mom!" I cheered. "Maybe I can take some time and come over to help you."

***

It was now the summer of 1989. Summer in the woods is lovely. Chuck hangs out on the upper sun deck of our home. From the second floor, he can see the many trees surrounding the back yard. He loves to watch the birds, although only Michael is able to mimic the sounds of the animals. I always supply bread, bits of cereal, and other treats for the wildlife in our area so our whole family can enjoy nature more closely. It was the beginning of a promising summer. Chuck's work was going well. I was feeling happier about my relationship with my mother, and my sons were enjoying a busy summer of karate, basketball, and tennis.

In July, Chuck left for a one-day trip to New York for several meetings. The kids had gone to camp, and I looked forward to a quiet day. Since I am a late riser, by the time I awoke, the ground was already saturated with rain. The birds chirped loudly. I knew it would rain all day long. When I climbed downstairs to my exercise room, I hadn't even opened the door before I heard the dripping sounds. I did not want to find out what was causing those sounds. As I entered the room, I saw the water dripping from several areas.

Luckily, we had many buckets. I placed the buckets all around the basement to catch the water. When they filled up, I carried the heavy buckets over to the sump pump. Between trips, I called the waterproofing company, but the man who answered the phone said, "Look, lady, you're not the only one. We got tons of complaints. We'll get to it as soon as we can." He told me to pray for the rain to stop. It didn't. All day I carried buckets and emptied buckets. Physically, I am not a very strong person, and I resented that this would happen when none of my men were home.

That night, I stopped to take a break. I was fixing myself some iced coffee. I reached for a spoon, and it slipped from my grasp. As I bent over to pick up the spoon, I heard something pop in my back. It was a sickening sound. Before I had time to figure out what had happened, I felt pain spreading throughout my body. It was excruciating. All I wanted to do was lie down. Maybe if I had a good sleep, when I awoke the pain would be gone. I rummaged in the medicine cabinet for something to help me fall asleep.

I must have been screaming because when I awoke, Chuck was holding me in his arms. It was four o'clock in the morning. I couldn't move, so Chuck called for an ambulance to rush me to the hospital.

At the hospital, I had several X-rays taken of my back. We anxiously awaited the results and were wonderfully relieved when the emergency doctor told us that there was nothing wrong with my back.

But my relief was short-lived. The next morning, I was not able to get out of bed by myself. I couldn't go to the bathroom by myself. I was in so much pain that I cried for hours.

When the pain did not ease, Chuck insisted that I visit our regular family doctor. Our doctor referred me to a specialist. Several doctors later, I discovered that I had a herniated disc in my spine. The specialist explained that this was a condition in which the gelatin within the disc slips out and presses against the nerve. The nerve then signals severe pain. When I asked whether the disc would heal, the doctor said it could heal, but he warned me that it would never quite return to normal.

For the next few months, I was bedridden and very miserable. I was not able to comfort my mother as I had planned, and she felt even more depressed when she heard how much I was suffering. If it had not been for my family, I honestly don't know how I would have made it. Chuck used to take me out of bed, bathe me, and then put me back in bed, interrupting his work day for my convenience.

Chuck adapted to catering to my physical needs; he found it painful to deal with my emotional needs. Chuck's mother never showed tears, so when I would cry every day over the seemingly endless pain, he really didn't know how to cope. My kids, who were raised by a mother who freely showed emotions, were better prepared to deal with me. Jarod and Michael would hug me. Sometimes, they would tickle my arms with a straw to relax me. They'd even wipe the tears from under my eyes. The boys were a role model for Chuck. Eventually, Chuck was able to deal with my emotions, and the three of them became an incredible wellness team. They showed me the importance of never giving up and toughing it out.

Months later, when I was well enough to walk, I began going to a physical therapist. The therapist put me on a traction device to help the healing process. For the rest of the summer, I continued doing traction and other exercises, such as pelvic tilts, in the comfort of my home.

Maybe it was because I was getting older, but I was determined to stop complaining and to make the best out of my painful situation. One of the things I learned from this injury is that we are all prisoners of our own bodies. In spite of all of the things that I wanted to do this summer, my body restrained me. I felt imprisoned by this unproductive body. Not only did my back injury ruin my summer, it prevented me from helping my mother.

Just about the time my disc popped, my mother prepared to move out of her big house and into a small apartment. After having given her the encouragement to clean out the house, I felt very guilty that I was useless to her now. My mother was in desperate need of help, and I was too incapacitated to even get out of bed.

Then, I reflected on the dream--the one that was slowly guiding my life for the better. In the last part of the dream, my parents needed me to bring in the stuff from the car, but I never did. Now, in real life, my mother needed me to help her move things out of the house, and I couldn't. All of a sudden, I didn't feel so bad. I realized that I wasn't supposed to help her because that is what the dream said. Every other part of the dream had come true, so I had to believe that this part had come true, also. The dream told me to cut her hands free and that was all. Then, for the first time, I understood the difference between what I had been doing to help my mother, and what I had to do to help her.

I continued to counsel my mother. First, I taught her how to date, although she hesitated about going out. I told her that being unhappy would not attract men. She soon found out that forcing herself to smile and to appear happy did indeed make her feel better as well as made her more attractive to others. Then, I taught her how to love a man and how to be loved--a feeling that was unknown to her. It was not easy for a woman in her seventies to adapt to a new lifestyle. Although my mother admitted that she was not really happy during her marriage, she was used to my father. He had been the only man she had dated seriously. How would she get used to someone else at her age? There was also the practical matter of too many widows for too few widowers.

But she wasn't the only one who needed counseling. She reminded me that I still hadn't forgiven my father. She told me that it wasn't healthy to go through life unable to forgive a parent.

"Look at your brother," she said. "Your brother has forgiven him, and now he has a better life. He's remarried. He has learned to love, and Larry and his second wife have a wonderful relationship."

I told my mother that I was not ready to forgive my father.

"I will worry about you until you find it in your heart to forgive him."

Even though I knew she was right, I was stuck in the past. I saw how her life improved after she forgave my father, and I had to admit that my brother was a happier person once he forgave my father. Now there was only me. Well, I simply couldn't. I was playing the game against my father, and I was still winning.

*** 

I could still hear my father's enraged voice when, on a Sunday afternoon drive, he missed the turn off the tollway and started to take it out on us. Only I seemed to be able to stop him from losing it completely. I was the apple of my daddy's eye. I think my father admired my inner strength because, in a way, it mirrored his own strength. I wanted a happy family so much! I did not want to settle for a dysfunctional home filled with violence, terror, and hatred.

I knew from a very early age that something was wrong, and I had trouble accepting that this was my real family. I remembered the times when I went outside at night to look at the stars. As I gazed at the night sky, I searched the heavens. Somewhere out there were my real parents. God must have accidentally mixed them up with these bad parents. My real parents were good, kind, and loving--the kind of people that I wanted to be like.

I can still picture myself being very scared before falling asleep at night. I would look at my bedroom ceiling and see colored dots everywhere. The dots came to life as they moved all around my ceiling. They frightened me when they jumped out at me. I used to hide my head under the pillow so they wouldn't get me.

The game I played with my father was one I designed to gain control over him. I saw how my mother and brother feared him and how he used that fear against them. I refused to let him scare me. Once when he was beating my brother with a belt, I dared him to beat me, too. "Hit me!"

I demanded. My father hesitated. I goaded him some more until he hit me. "Hit me again--that didn't hurt!" He hit me so hard I almost fell over, but I had won the game. I was relieved that the next time my mother called, she did not bring up the subject of forgiving my father.

Instead, she mentioned that she began to engage socially with a few friends. She told me how it seemed that all the pieces of my psychic dream played out in real life. She told me that she believed in my dream and that, through the dream, she understood why I was compelled to help her.

"Your grandmother had psychic dreams as well," she reminded me.

"Tell me about them, " I begged her.

"Your grandmother immigrated to the United States before I was born. All of her relatives were already in the States, except for one family. She never talked much about that family, yet one night she dreamt that this family wanted to come to the United States very much, but they were not able to because they were missing a certain amount of money. The dream also showed her how much money they needed. On a hunch that the dream might actually be true, you grandmother went around to all of the relatives, even though they themselves were poor, to ask for donations. As it turned out, she collected the exact amount of money that she dreamt the family needed to come over. Then, she sent the money overseas. Indeed, it was the exact amount that this family needed in order to be able to come over. The family was happily reunited with all the other relatives because of your grandmother and her dream."

***

As I began to live with my back, I poured more time into helping Chuck build our business. Together we developed strategies on how to use our accomplishments to our advantage in attracting new clients and putting together bigger and bigger deals. In 1990, L.A. Gear peaked at nine hundred million dollars, which was well above the half-billion figure that Robert Greenberg had originally predicted. Apparel Connections International's track record with L.A. Gear brought us to a new level of respect in the industry.

As Chuck's reputation grew, people began to recommend him as a licensing agent. He was now representing a top modeling agency, Nancy Reagan's "Just Say No" Foundation, Cigarette racing boats, and the National Troopers Coalition to which state troopers throughout the country belong. A mutual friend referred Steve Banarjee, the owner of the Chippendales, to Chuck. One of the first products Chuck arranged to license was a poster of the male Chippendale dancers. Later, Chuck successfully incorporated pictures of the Chippendales into little hand-held movie viewers.

One day, Chuck received a complaint regarding the viewers. The Marriott Hotel Chain purchased hundreds of these viewers for its gift shops which were set up in rest areas on the turnpikes. The Marriott Corporation was founded by Mormons who firmly believe in family values. Imagine the surprise of the Marriott managers when, upon opening the boxes of viewers, they found not the cute Chip 'n Dale viewer they had expected, but viewers featuring the Chippendale strippers!

Still, despite these minor setbacks, Apparel Connections International continued to grow. Spending more time developing the business enabled me to distract myself from my back injury. As I had promised myself, I spent less time complaining. Then, slowly but surely, I started to recuperate.

## Chapter 3

Throughout my whole life, I've felt as though something or someone higher than a human being was guiding me to make the right decisions for myself. I called these my spirit guides, and I consulted them every day while I was exercising. I showed them appreciation for everything they had done so far and asked them for help when I needed it. I took them into my heart as if they were lifelong friends that would never leave my side.

Sometime in my twenties, I was taught a method of deriving answers to any questions I might have about myself. All I had to do was to create a person in my mind-- a person whom I could see clearly. The person I visualized would answer my question.

Now I needed to create a new person. One day when the house was quiet, I put myself into a trance by closing my eyes and blocking out everything. I was transformed somewhere else. Would it work? As I continued to concentrate, I saw myself walking over a bridge, through a tropical forest, and around a bend until I came to a shack. I could tell by the coconut trees and the sky blue water that I was on a Caribbean island.

Something drew me inside the shack. Once I adjusted my eyes to the semi-darkness, I saw an old woman sitting on a hard wooden bench. She was in her nineties and all alone in the shack. The woman dressed all in white. She was very pretty, and she looked just like me except that she was skinny and haggard-looking. Her long hair was snow white and combed back--unlike my hair which is long and brown and worn in bangs.

Our relationship seemed distant, but not cold. I suppose I could compare it to the first time you meet your best friend--only you don't know it yet. Obviously, there is some distance until you begin to know and trust one another, but all along you've felt a unique bond with that person. This is how I first felt about the old lady in the shack. She wasn't cold or uninviting, yet when I would ask her a question about myself, the business, or anything else, she always said something like, "Why not?" She wouldn't answer me with specifics, only with vague answers that I knew I would have to figure out on my own.

One question I didn't have to ask the old woman was whether I would miss my older son Jarod when he went off to college. I already knew. When we sent Jarod to college at the end of the summer, Chuck and I felt confident that Jarod had selected a good school, George Washington University, where he had been granted an academic scholarship. Jarod had no problem making friends, and, as far as protection was concerned, he had earned a black belt in karate. We were worried not so much for our son but for ourselves. After all, Jarod's departure marked the very first time our tight-knit family unit would be separated, and Chuck and I didn't know how to handle it.

The night before Jarod left, Chuck, Michael, and I got together and let out our feelings. We cried right in front of Jarod. Then, we took him to school, came back, and cried some more. We each knew that we had to learn to get over this loss in our own way. I felt very empty. Parents go through a lot raising their children, and when a child is ready to try his own wings, it's hard to let go. After Jarod left, each night before I went to sleep, I tiptoed into his bedroom to gaze at his high school prom picture to remind myself that he had left the nest.

As much as I missed my son, I didn't want to be the kind of mother who could never let go. I had to find another focus for my attention. Then, I found it--my attention would be directed to Linda Gilman and the problem of getting herself back into shape.

I was grateful that my back was gradually feeling better. I began to exercise more. Every day I rode my stationary bike for ten miles. After that, I used our Universal System to begin a weight-lifting program. I started to feel better about my appearance, and, at the same time, I was getting my mind to focus on other things. I had to admit that raising kids properly was an incredible burden. But no matter what a mother does, her kids will be gone someday, and all she has left is herself and, hopefully, her husband.

Chuck needed me in many ways, but he didn't need a mother. Chuck and I have a good working relationship despite the fact that we're in the house together all day long. Chuck is an early riser. When he gets up, he uses the gym in our basement during the morning hours. Then, by the time I wake up, he is done exercising and it's time for lunch. During our lunch, we talk. This is our time to discuss whatever is going on in the business or to share gossip. We do playful characters together, and we talk about serious issues together. Then, it's my turn to use the gym throughout the afternoon while Chuck is in his office. While I'm on my bike, I usually talk to my mother, to Carol, or to other close friends. Each day, I devote this time to mutual therapy. Our differing schedules enable Chuck and me to give each other space, even though we are in the same house day and night. The end result is a more passionate and loving relationship than either of us ever could have imagined.

I continued to counsel my mother and, as a result, she began to come out of her shell. Once she got the house fixed up and ready for sale, she seemed to be more light-hearted. Even her voice, which always had a whining tone to it, took on a certain pleasantness. She had met a nice man at a senior social and was dating again. Of course, she missed Jarod, too, and we often talked about funny things Jarod had done when he was younger.

For example, whenever Jarod had been punished and sent to his room, he was always let out within the first five minutes. He would use his amazing writing skills and deliver a message to me by way of a paper airplane. His messages would always melt my heart. When the boys were little, Jarod used to entertain Michael for hours by writing stories that made them both hysterical. Remembering these stories was one of the ways I overcame the void of Jarod's absence.

Jarod called frequently from school. He was always bubbling with news, and although he said he missed us, I knew he had found a new home. His holiday visits seemed very short. His first report card showed that he had chosen the right school and that he was on his way to success, so I could no longer make him an excuse for not going ahead with new phases of my own life.

\*\*\*

Towards the end of the Gulf War in April of 1991, I made my own peace with myself. Since I had exercised all year long, I now was proud of the way I looked--except that when I started to try on sexier summer bathing suits that came up higher on my legs, I noticed that ugly scar from the surgery I had undergone when I was four years old. The scar was now very thick and quite noticeable in these new bathing suits. I had heard that it was possible to have scars thinned out through plastic surgery, so I figured that if this scar was going to get in the way of my feeling good about myself, it had to go. At the same time, I would be able to get rid of four moles that had always annoyed me. I made the decision to have the scar thinned.

At this time, Pam and I experienced control issues that interfered with our relationship, and we drifted apart. As Pam exited my life, a new friend--Janet--entered my life, and we became close very quickly. Unlike myself, Janet is very outgoing. She was exploring ways of using her singing talent and performed for a number of groups and organizations. Janet told me that her last engagement was at a nursery school. While she was entertaining, she ran into my old friend Caren.

Caren and I had been friends in our twenties and I had helped her through many tough times in her life. Janet told Caren that she was close with me and asked Caren whether she wanted to renew an old friendship. When Caren said, "yes," Janet acted as the go-between.

Someone once told me true friends will always be friends even after they haven't seen each other for years. When I called Caren, it was like old times. We discussed everything, including the surgery on my scar, called adhesion revision, that I was about to undergo. As Caren and I made plans to get together, she told me that she had some information about the procedure that she would share with me when we met for dinner.

At the dinner, Caren listened carefully to my problem and then recommended a plastic surgeon named Barry Kramer. I didn't know it at the time, but in telling me the name of this surgeon, I believe that she was returning a karmic favor to me. In other words, she was destined to give me this information. After meeting with Caren a few more times, we slowly drifted apart again, but she left me with the key which would eventually open the door to my soul.

I called the practice of Kramer and Reed to make an appointment with Dr. Barry Kramer. I made it at a time when Chuck would be able to go with me. While we were waiting in Dr. Kramer's Center City, Philadelphia office, a woman entered the room. She seemed to know the office routine, and so I assumed this wasn't her first visit. After a while, I leaned over to ask her what she thought of Dr. Kramer. She told me that he performed major surgery on her just seven months ago.

"My dear, he did such a good job on me! I would never let anyone else touch me again."

Just then, a tall, dark-haired doctor greeted us. He had an engaging, open manner about him which immediately put both Chuck and me at ease. I was glad that he didn't just talk about the upcoming surgery, but that he talked about current events and made me feel like a real person and not just another surgery case. He even discussed all the problems associated with being a doctor in today's times, including the high costs of medical malpractice insurance. I had been in contact with many doctors during my life, but this doctor was different. He had a certain charisma which reminded me of Robert Greenberg.

Our next visits were also enjoyable. The three of us were making jokes, and we all got along incredibly well. On one visit, I remember Chuck telling one joke that I thought was hilarious. Although he laughed at the other jokes, Dr. Kramer just shrugged it off. During a later visit,

Dr. Kramer, with whom we were now on a first name basis, mentioned to us that he had thought about that certain joke as he stepped into his shower at home, and he could not stop laughing. This delayed reaction clued me into the fact that Barry was a thinker and the type of person who carries his thoughts around with him rather than dropping them before he has a chance to fully digest their meaning.

As the day of the surgery drew closer, I began to have second thoughts. Just to make sure I should go ahead, I decided to consult the old woman who I now referred to as the Old Lady. I went over the bridge, through the forest, around the bend, and into her shack.

"Should I have my scar fixed, and will I be okay afterwards?" I asked her.

"I did it," she replied. Somehow, I knew this meant that I would be fine in the end.

At last the day of the surgery arrived, and I went in as scheduled. Barry did everything as planned. What happened next, though, was not planned. When the surgery was over, Barry tried to wake me up, but I would not respond. He tried again, but it was no use--I still would not come to. Now, I have had many surgeries, and I never had a problem waking up after the operation. Finally, after the fourth time, Barry was able to get me to regain consciousness. Only when I woke up, it was not in my head where people usually become alert. I woke up in my stomach. It felt very strange to me...as if I had left my body and now was returning through my stomach. I stayed in my stomach until I fully regained consciousness. This was a sensation unlike any I had ever experienced. The only possible explanation to me was that perhaps I wasn't really there when Barry tried to wake me up. Maybe I had an out-of-body experience.

Something else went wrong with the surgery, although it was not Barry's fault. When Barry made the cut on top of my scar, the entire area from my stomach all the way down my leg became covered in bruises. My stomach, my vagina, and my upper thigh turned bright red. Barry explained to me that this was a freak accident traced to the cut the doctors made in 1951 during the surgery performed on me when I was four years old.

***

The cause of my first surgery was a bike accident. When I was little, we lived on a crowded block right next to a busy highway. My brother and I used to ride our bikes around the whole block together. Larry had a two-wheeler, and I had a tricycle. He used to take his toy rifle with him when we pedaled around our block, and we would have races, too. My brother always let me win because he was eight and I was only four--he was much bigger in size.

One day, he had gotten too much of a lead and, afraid that he might win, he dropped his rifle on purpose and screamed to me, "Go faster, Linda! Go faster! You can beat me!" I pedaled as fast as my short legs could. Then, as I neared the corner where the little street ran into the highway, I looked back to see how far ahead I was. By that time, I was going too fast to make the turn. As I lost control, I flipped over my bike and, luckily, landed on the side street instead of on the busy highway.

But, then, I wasn't so lucky. As I was falling off, the handle bar of the bike pushed deep into my groin. It hurt so much that I couldn't move. When I started to cry, my brother put me on his bike and wheeled me home.

Later that night while my mother gave me a bath, I

coughed and out popped a lump from my lower abdomen. My mother was petrified and took me over to a doctor. The doctor said I had a rupture and a hernia and that I'd have to be operated on immediately.

***

Now forty years later, the surgery caused more complications. Because of these complications, Barry thought it was better that I stay overnight in the hospital. That night at approximately twelve-thirty, Barry stopped by the hospital after a meeting in order to check on me. Finding me asleep, he had the nurse wake me up. Then, he reached behind me to wrap a gauze rope around the bed post. He instructed me to pull on it if I wanted the light turned on. I began to play with this gauze rope when all of a sudden I got a funny feeling inside. I didn't know what it was, though.

Then, we started to talk about the surgery. I asked him why my body was so sensitive to the cut, and he said it was because I am delicate. He told me I was like the princess in the story of the princess and the pea. Suddenly, the funny feeling came back. I was remembering something from my childhood, but I didn't quite know what it was. The only thing I did know was that my father used to call me a princess, and Barry's comment made me think of my father. Even worse, Barry's wrapping the gauze rope around the bed post caused me to remember the same type of gauze rope that the nurses threatened to tie me up with after my surgery when I was four.

***

After the doctor told my parents that I needed an

operation, my parents took me to the hospital immediately. I really didn't understand what was going on. The nurses told me I could have a private room, and I remember being happy because my other choice was a children's ward where all the kids who couldn't afford a private room had to stay. The nurses put me in a private room. Then, they informed me that my parents were not allowed to stay with me. At that point, I screamed at the top of my lungs. The nurses immediately took me out of the room and put me in the ward.

As soon as I entered the ward, I noticed that things were not right. Some of the kids were being tied up with gauze rope because they weren't behaving right or because they weren't sleeping in the right position. The nurses threatened to tie me up just for screaming. Right from the beginning, I hated everything about the place.

The very next day, they performed surgery on me. When I woke up from the operation, I felt a terrible burning sensation on my right side from my vagina all the way up to my stomach. I was just opening my eyes when I saw a man between my legs. He was putting medicine on me when I realized that I was completely naked. I was so angry that I closed my eyes, pretending to be asleep. Slowly, I pulled back my left foot, took aim, and kicked him right in the face with all of my strength. It was a perfect kick, and I knew that I had hit the target. Then, I went loose on this man, kicking him and screaming at him until all the nurses had to come in and hold me down. It didn't matter. I had made my point.

After the surgery, I was put back in that ward for ten more days. They didn't treat me right in the ward, and I knew it even at the age of four. One of the nurses was very mean. She used to wake me up by scrubbing my face with a wet rag.  Other nurses would come around to the ward each day to give enemas to all the kids.  When it was the older kids' turns, and especially when it was the boys' turns, the nurses made sure to close the curtains so nobody could see.  But when it was my turn, they decided that they didn't need to close the curtain because I was only four and probably hadn't experienced feelings of shame or embarrassment yet.  Well, when they gave me the enema and then put me on the potty seat in front of all the boys and girls, I was devastated.  I had never been so embarrassed in my short four-year life.

At this point, I declared war on that hospital!  The only sure way of getting them angry was by refusing to eat, so that's just what I did.  When the nurses would carry in trays of food, I would just look away.  I refused to eat.  The only food I ate was my mother's home-cooked food, and that was only because she would promise to take me home afterwards.  She made this promise every day, but every night she would leave without me when visiting hours were over.

Between my crying and not eating, I was getting smaller and smaller and smaller.  One of my aunts came to visit me on the first day after my operation.  She brought me a very large doll.  By the end of the ten days, I had gotten so small that I could fit into the doll's clothes.  My weight loss was getting very serious, but I didn't care.  No matter what, I would not let them win.

***

When I married, I was determined to block out most of my childhood.  My father was an abusive man.  He used to physically and emotionally abuse my mother and my brother constantly. Yet, he treated people outside the family wonderfully. He was well-respected by his customers and by the community. But our home was dysfunctional and filled with violence, terror, and hatred--a home from which I felt I had no escape. When I married Chuck, I created a new family that had love and compassion.

My life was patterned after the Chinese Yin-Yang symbol where good and evil live together. The good of my life began when I moved out of my original home at the age of twenty-two. The evil was my life up to that point. But what I didn't realize was that the two segments of my life actually live side by side, just like the symbol indicates. Although I was able to block out the evil from my conscious mind during my good adult life, the evil from the past was still there, hidden deep within me. As I tried to recover from my second surgery, the evil memories began to seep into my conscious mind for the very first time...and it didn't feel good.

Although I had never really thought much about numerology, Janet began to point out the significance of numbers in our lives. After I convinced her that the number four seemed to be a dominant motif in my life, she realized that my name also worked out to a four. When I asked her what four meant, Janet explained that it refers to the basic life processes. She also remembered talking to a psychic once who said that the number four represents power.

We reviewed the fours in my life: my childhood surgery took place at age four; my second surgery occurred at age forty-four; the two surgeries were exactly forty years apart; and the most recent surgery was dated April 24, the twenty-fourth day of the fourth month.

"There's a pattern!" I insisted.

The next time I called my mother, I asked her the date of my childhood surgery. My mother stopped to think. Then, she said that my accident happened on Easter Sunday.

"Then when was my surgery?" I persisted. She said that the surgery was a few days after that.

"Then it must have been in April?" I asked.

"Yes," she confirmed.

After telling her about the fours, I said, "Mother, April is the fourth month of the year!" I knew that this was not a coincidence. I thanked her for the information. As I was hanging up, it occurred to me that I removed four moles during my adult surgery, and Barry tried to wake me four times before I finally gained consciousness. More fours!

That night, I decided to tell Chuck about he fours. I told him that all of these fours were popping up everywhere.

"Chuck, there has to be something to this," I asserted. Chuck looked at me disappointedly.

"Linda, you have nothing better to do with your time than notice all these fours?" I knew he was very frustrated with me. Usually Chuck tried to be patient with me, and sometimes he even attempted to be open-minded, but numerology asked him to cross the boundary established by his logical mind. Chuck wanted proof, but I only had evidence of the possibility. He didn't buy it. Despite Chuck's skepticism, I knew there had to be some significance in the number four.

I also was fascinated by the connection between the two surgeries. I couldn't help thinking that when Barry had cut me, he had cut into my memory bank because all the horrid memories of my four-year old surgery flared up. I had awakened from my stomach. Could my stomach be the vault where all the memories were stored?  Since leaving the hospital, I felt an imaginary ball growing inside my stomach.  If I hadn't known better, I would have thought that I was pregnant.  The ball was alive, and it was slowly getting bigger.  I could feel it even if I couldn't understand it.

What was wrong with me?  I had an imaginary ball growing inside of me, and I was getting depressed over something that happened forty years ago.  Could all of this be the result of my surgery?  Why couldn't I have a normal surgery like everybody else?  I felt like I had all the pieces of a jigsaw puzzle in front of me, but I had lost the box cover that has the picture of what the puzzle should look like.

# Chapter 4

The first weekend after my surgery, Chuck ran into Barry Kramer and his wife, Myrna, at a gas station. When Chuck came home, he told me that they seemed like such a nice couple, and we ought to take them out to dinner sometime. I was hesitant. Of course, we both knew Barry, but that was because he was my doctor. I had never met Myrna, and even though Chuck thought that she was pleasant, I felt we would be intruding. I was still Barry's patient. But Chuck persisted. He was surprised that I resisted the idea. I tried to explain to Chuck that I believe there are certain social rules you should live by, and while we all got along great in the office, I would be breaking a social rule that doctors should not mix after hours with their patients.

Chuck did not agree. "Linda," he said, "you know I respect your viewpoint, but I have never been the type of person who is restrained by social rules. If I like the person, then I think I have a right to ask that person out and to form a friendship."

I couldn't deny that this works for Chuck because it is how he operates in the business world. However, I lived a more reclusive life at this point, and I thought differently.

When Carol came over that afternoon, I told her about Chuck's accidental meeting with the Kramers and asked her opinion. She said that if Chuck really wished to invite them out, she didn't think it was wrong because if they didn't want to go, they could always make an excuse for not going with us.

Later that summer of 1991, Chuck and I saw the movie, The Doctor, starring William Hurt. The movie is about a doctor who is cold and apathetic towards his patients, but he gets a taste of his own medicine when he gets sick himself. That's when the doctor sees firsthand how insensitive doctors can be. All of a sudden, I began to miss Barry. I remembered how kind and caring he was to me even though I was only at the hospital for minor surgery. At this point, I considered that it wouldn't be such a bad idea to go out with Barry and his wife after all.

One more person came to my mind as someone who would think about my dilemma seriously. I called my friend Mary Ann who is married to a surgeon. She spoke to her husband about it, and he said that although it's not common for doctors and patients to see each other socially, he thought it was a wonderful idea.

While I now was warming up to the idea, I couldn't act on it yet. There was a lot going on in our lives. Chuck's business was booming more than ever. L.A. Gear approached the billion dollar mark aided by a one hundred million dollar investment, primarily from the Disney family. After a two year hold on licensing, Robert Greenberg called Chuck to ask him to rebuild L.A. Gear's licensing program. Also, America's top modeling agency was now using Chuck's services. In addition, Chuck and I were busy getting Jarod ready for his second year at college. But I still kept an open mind towards the idea of socializing with Barry and Myrna.

It was the end of the summer of 1991, and we had to face bringing Jarod back to school. We were going to help him move into his new room at the fraternity house. I still had not gotten over Jarod's leaving for college, and his second departure gave me additional doubts as to what I should be doing with the rest of my life. Of course, I already knew that my life was getting stranger and stranger. But I wasn't worried for myself, I was worried for Jarod.

When we got to the university and saw the condition of the fraternity house, I knew I had been right to worry. I felt sick to my stomach from the filth and foul odors. Chuck said it looked like it hadn't been cleaned in years. Michael, in his take-charge way, started to clean. He fixed the broken door and started unpacking the clothes. Regardless of the conditions, Jarod was obligated to live there for one year. Jarod would share the burden with fifteen other fraternity brothers. Their parents felt the same way about the house as Chuck and me. We unloaded all of Jarod's belongings from the rental van, and we stayed in Washington for the entire weekend.

As the three of us went home on Interstate 95, we heard on the radio that a big storm was approaching. Then, minutes later, the rental van started to make a choking sound like it was losing its power. There was an exit on the right side of the highway. As soon as I noticed it, an overwhelming thought entered my head. It said very loudly, "Get off the highway and go to the right." I blurted the message to Chuck. He resisted.

"Linda, there are state troopers going back and forth patrolling the highway. If we get off the highway, they won't be able to help us. We would be in the middle of nowhere."

I refused to listen to his logic. Now, I was screaming for him to get off the highway. Instead of fighting with me, which would have been futile at this point, he pulled over to the exit and started to slow down once we reached the new road.

"Don't stop," I told him. "Keep going to the right." Even though Chuck knew I have no sense of direction, he listened. As we were speeding up again, the van made all kinds of noises, and then it started to slow down by itself.

Chuck was right--we were smack dab in the middle of nowhere. Had I made a mistake?

Suddenly, a gas station appeared. Luckily, the van had just enough power to coast right onto the lot of the gas station. It died just short of the gas pump.

While Chuck was looking it over, we could hear police cars and fire engines headed in our direction. The police drove up to the van.

"Get out of that van immediately!" one of them ordered. We did as we were told. The police officer went on to explain. "There is a fire burning beneath your van," he told us. He said that he noticed it as we were getting off the exit ramp. He radioed ahead for fire trucks and additional police cars in case the whole van should catch fire. Thank God that by the time we pulled into the gas station, the fire had burned out.

The police officer called a cab for us, and we were able to make it home safely that night. However, had I not screamed at Chuck to pull off at the exit because of the overwhelmingly loud thought in my head, we would have been stranded on the highway or, worse yet, enveloped in flames. That night, I thanked my spirit guides for helping me.

Jarod was in school. Chuck was closing some of the biggest deals of his career. Now that everything was under control, I figured that it was time to start thinking about getting together with Barry and Myrna. But before Chuck could phone them, I had to overcome my fear of rejection. I was threatened by Chuck's association with a new level of people. Why would these people want to spend time with me?

***

Growing up in one of the few Jewish families in an all gentile neighborhood made me sensitive to rejection, and it didn't help that I was shy by nature. My mother always felt that my shyness would create problems for me as I got older, so she tried to help me in her own way.

Every day, my mother would force me to come downstairs to the pharmacy and talk to people in the store. At first, I used to hide behind her skirt. I wouldn't show my face. One day, an old man who leaned on a crutch peaked around my mother's skirt and hollered, "Peek-a-boo, I see you!" I laughed so hard that I sat on the floor. Then, the man said, "A pretty girl like you should never hide."

After a while, talking to people came easier, and eventually I could converse with almost anyone. Still, even to this day, I am scared to initiate talks with anyone I don't know because I always think that they won't like me.

\*\*\*

When I married Chuck, I never dreamed that we would be going into the deal-making business. When we did, I realized that Chuck and I had two obstacles to conquer-- jealousy and fear of rejection. The jealousy would stem from the fact that in order to succeed in business, we would have to be with people who were wealthier than we were. We would have to deal with people whose lives were more interesting and more fun than ours. I would have to associate with women much prettier than me. I made up my mind that whenever Chuck and I would get these feelings of jealousy, we would have to combat them or else we would never make any progress at all.

Gradually, I developed a system of thought that both of

us have used.  It is based on the following concept:  I know that my day would not change one bit if someone else's day was better.  If one of Chuck's business associates is relaxing on a yacht while I am at home working, then although that person is having a great time, it has absolutely no effect on my day.  I want to be the best I can be, but if I let myself worry about the fact that other people's lives seem better than mine, I will only feel let down.  The truth is that I, too, want to be on that yacht eventually, but negative thinking is not going to get me there.

The other obstacle that we had to conquer was rejection. Rejection is the nature of Chuck's business, so he learned to face rejection firsthand on a daily basis.  Then, I would feel the rejection through him.  Again, I developed a thought system for Chuck to use.  I told Chuck to think about how it would change his day if he gets rejected.

I said, "Let's say you are walking through a trade show. You approach a company that looks like one you would be interested in doing business with, but the company says it's not interested.  Does this mean that you won't brush your teeth before you go to bed that night?  No, it doesn't.  In fact, you will go to bed that night, and you will wake up to the same routine the next day."

I told him that rejection wouldn't change a thing. Chuck listened to me because he knew I was right. However, I never entirely conquered rejection myself.  As much as I could tell him how to overcome this fear, I was still its slave because I didn't have to face it head-on like he did.  I was protected by a very sheltered life with the same group of supportive friends, so the need to master my fear did not arise frequently.

I tried to remember how I used to go out to make friends when I was a little girl.  Since I was a typical tomboy, I didn't like traditional girl things. But I was so good at baseball that every time I played on the boys' team, I was chosen to be the pitcher, the most important position on the team. In a way, playing sports enabled me to escape from my family. When I was on a team, everybody liked me. Not only was I one of the best on the team, but I was also the only girl playing with all boys--and that in itself carried with it a great deal of respect. I was also an object of neighborhood curiosity.

I decided to tell Carol about my feelings of rejection. She said she thought that everyone had some anxieties about being rejected. According to Carol, even her husband whose outgoing personality made him a top salesman was "impossible" after he faced a day of rejection.

"Carol, I have to tell you a funny story." I loved to tell her stories of my childhood because I knew she enjoyed them. Of all my friends, Carol's life was most similar to mine. Besides, we think alike on most issues. I told Carol about the time the boys decided to start a special club where one of the rites of passage was having to pull down your pants. Not only was I the only girl, but I was very self-conscious about the big scar near my groin. I knew I would be embarrassed if I had to pull down my pants, so I decided to be sneaky. I just stood there and watched as all the little boys exposed their Dangling Johnsons. Then, when it was my turn, I started to reach for my pants--and then I turned and ran as fast as I could. Naturally, the boys couldn't chase after me with their pants around their ankles, so I got away. Carol laughed and laughed at my story.

Then, she asked me if my brother Larry liked sports, too.

"No," I answered. "Larry was more interested in hobbies." I told her how my father wanted his son to be more athletic. My father thought that by abusing my brother, he could make a man out of him.

"Your father must have been really proud of you," said Carol.

"Yeah, but I didn't care. All I cared about was that sports introduced me to the world of boys."

That's when Carol confided in me that she had been Ron Perelman's girlfriend for five years when she was a teenager. "You mean Ron Perelman who owns Revlon?"

"Yes," she answered.

"Carol, he is one of the richest men in the world--I just read about him in Chuck's business magazine!"

Carol switched the conversation to Barry and Myrna, asking if we had made arrangements to go out with them. "No," I confessed. "I haven't gotten up the nerve to ask." I admitted to her that I really wanted to make friends with Barry and his wife because of everything that Barry did for me. Carol looked at me directly.

"You must get over your fear," she said sternly.

That night, I asked Chuck to call Barry because I was too scared. I even gave Chuck a line to use at the beginning of the conversation. He could ask Barry if he had a problem going out with his patients. This way, if Barry really didn't want to go out with us, then he could say "yes" to Chuck's question, and I wouldn't have to feel the sting of rejection.

But my fears were for nothing. As soon as Chuck called, Barry accepted our invitation. I was thrilled! Chuck told me that he gave Barry a choice of three dates in the near future. Barry informed Chuck that he was going to be very busy during the next few weeks, but he would have Myrna give me a call to confirm a date. Well, the three dates came and went, and I still hadn't heard from Myrna.

I told Chuck that Myrna probably didn't want to go out with us. Chuck kept telling me that Barry sounded like he had a smile on his face when they spoke. But I couldn't help feeling confused, so off I went to visit the Old Lady. When I asked her if Myrna was going to call me, she said, "Of course," and I knew to let it go and eventually Myrna would call. Finally, after a couple of weeks passed, Myrna did call. She began by saying that it wasn't necessary for us to take them out. I said that we'd love to. Then, she said she would love to join us, so we made a date. I was very happy that she called.

The Friday night that we went out to dinner, we invited them to our house first for wine and cheese. Because they live in the same township, it didn't take them long to drive over. I wanted to show them what we were all about, and I also wanted them to know that we were substantial people, just as they were. They came to our house an hour late because their little boy was sick. I felt bad, so I gave them a little gift to take home to their son. I dug up a pair of Teenage Mutant Ninja Turtle slippers, one of the many sample products that are sent to Chuck from companies seeking to do business with him. Then, we went to dinner.

At dinner, we laughed and talked the whole time. We got along wonderfully with each other. Despite my earlier reservations, I had no indication that they hadn't wanted to be with us. Myrna told us a story during dinner that I thought was hysterical. She happened to be in Barry's office one day when a woman came up to her. In a very snotty tone of voice, the woman said, "I don't have to worry about the bill because we're good friends with the doctor and his wife. In fact, we were just out with them Saturday night, and Barry said I didn't have to pay for it."

Myrna patiently waited until the woman finished.

49

Then, she said, "Look, lady, I am the doctor's wife, and I don't recall being with you on Saturday night." With that, the woman paid her bill.

We all shared funny stories, and we were becoming very relaxed with one another. The only tension I felt was when Barry and Myrna sparred with each other, which was quite often. They did a good job of concealing their anger, but I could tell that Barry wasn't acting the same way he had in his office.

Halfway through dinner, while Myrna was talking to Chuck, I told Barry something very flattering. I told him that he had a lot of talent and charisma and that he was special to me. Then, I said there was another man in our lives named Robert Greenberg who I felt the same way about. I explained to Barry that both he and Robert had similar types of charisma about them and that they both did wonderful things for me. Robert gave us stock options and helped make our business successful, and Barry fixed something that had bothered me all of my life. When I finished, he smiled at me. It wasn't much of a reaction, but at least he was letting me know that he was happy to hear this.

That night, I also told him that I am psychic. Without very much emotion, he asked, "Are you?" It was almost as if the enchanting and delightful personality from his office disappeared for the evening.

"Yes, I am." I reaffirmed.

Then he turned to Chuck. "Is she?" he asked.

Now, at the time, Chuck still could not use the word "psychic" to describe me. He would say that there was a fine line between psychic and normal, but he admitted that I had some kind of extra-sensory perception. When Chuck said this, I made a decision not to talk about my psychic dream but to describe my ESP instead. I felt like my ESP would interest Barry just the same, and I really didn't want to turn him off in case he didn't believe in psychic occurrences.

I said to Barry, "I can be somebody else."

He asked, "Does that mean you know that person's strengths and weaknesses?"

"No," I answered, but I explained that I can protect that person. I told him that I naturally liked to protect people. "I think this might be because I always had to protect my mother and my brother from my father." I told him that I couldn't be sure where this desire came from.

"But I know that the reason I'm able to protect people is because I can foresee what consequences will result from certain actions. In other words, I will say to someone, 'If you do this, then this will happen.' If the consequence is good, then I encourage the action. If it is bad, I discourage it."

I explained that it is a special gift I have, and I know it works because I have been protecting myself all my life.

Later, Barry talked about Myrna and said that she likes to "yo-yo" people. I didn't understand what he meant, but I felt that he was trying to protect me with his remark.

The next day around noontime, Myrna called me to thank me for the dinner. I was still asleep, which is my normal pattern, when she called. When I called her back and told her why I didn't answer the phone, I could tell that my reason did not sit well with her. She was very surprised that I slept so late. Then, after I mentioned the idea of Myrna and I going out for dinner sometime, she started to yell about how she stayed home with her kids for dinner and, if her friends can't understand that, they aren't really her friends.

Since I did not mean to upset her with the invitation, I determined that she had a great deal of anger inside of her. Obviously, it was so close to the surface that it was starting to spill over.

"That's all right," I said calmly, "I have other friends to go out with." Then, she began to back down. I certainly was receiving mixed signals from her.

As the conversation continued, we were civil to each other. We even made plans to go out to dinner with both our families. The date we picked was during Jarod's winter break from college. We chose January 3, 1992. Just before we ended our conversation, Myrna said, "When Barry and I go out, we like to have fun."

Now, I had absolutely no clue as to what she meant by that comment. Was she telling me that we showed them lots of fun the night before, or was she implying that we didn't show them enough fun? Or, was she telling me it was our job to show them lots of fun in the future? All I could be sure of was that I suddenly felt pressure to show them fun the next time we went out.

# Chapter 5

It was now wintertime, my least favorite season of the year. I looked outside the kitchen window. The trees were bare; the skies were grey, and the birds had flown south for the winter. Of course, I still had the squirrels and raccoons to feed. Michael was now a sophomore in high school and was becoming very popular with the kids in his youth group. He constantly had a phone glued to his ear. Jarod was doing well in school. He was living in the fraternity house and enjoying the fraternity parties on the weekends. Although the filthy house was slightly improved, Jarod still had to hold an open umbrella over his head to protect himself from the upstairs leaks when he used the John.

Janet was singing and getting better bookings for her performances. Carol was beginning to socialize with a few new couples that she and her husband had met at their country club. I was feeling status quo, except for the ball growing inside me.

Who could I talk to about an imaginary ball? My mother had finally settled into her new apartment and was making friends with the other widows in her building. She was truly rebuilding her life. How could I bother my mother with the tale of the imaginary ball?

Someone once told me that good friends are like jewels. Each one is unique with her own beautiful facets. Pam was tall and attractive. To someone who didn't know her well, she could seem aloof. But once she accepted your friendship, she was down to earth and lots of fun. Although we had gone through rough times together as our husbands made career changes, we still weren't ready to renew our friendship. My friend Mary Ann has always been a very loyal and devoted friend. I felt a real loss when she moved to California to be with her new husband.

When I told Janet about the ball growing inside of me, she admitted that she had never heard of such a thing. She told me what I had described to her was very interesting and it definitely was significant, but I could not immediately figure out what it was trying to tell me.

As we spoke, I suggested that maybe this ball was a sort of pregnancy that had something to do with my inner child. Janet agreed that the inner child lives within everyone--it is the part of our being that refuses to grow up. It has a purity unclouded by the negative experiences of adulthood. Then, she recommended that I watch a new television series which would run on Channel 12, an educational channel. It was a course on the inner child given by John Bradshaw. When I told Janet that I had never heard of him, she told me that she had read several of his books. Janet went on to explain how our inner child becomes wounded by not having all of our childhood needs met. Janet told me that John Bradshaw spent many years of his life developing and researching this human condition. After reading his books, Janet felt that she gained some of the most valuable information she had ever learned. She convinced me that sampling the program for an evening could benefit me. At the very least, I would waste a couple of hours. I promised to watch.

I am not the kind of person who asks for help and then refuses to accept it, so I kept my promise. I became very involved in the program, and I watched this course for three hours a night, every night for a whole week. Although I was enjoying the program, it bothered me. It seemed as though my own inner child was waking up. Many of my childhood memories were returning. Since these were painful memories, I wasn't sure that I wanted them.

One memory was of the hostage game my father used to play with me. In this game, my father would take my mother hostage and make her life miserable so I would give up and do what he wanted me to do. Although I had a strong urge to protect her, I would never bend. I had the attitude of a nation which would rather sacrifice a few hostages than submit to hostile demands. If he was going to kill her to try to win me over, then he would have to kill her. In effect, I was emotionally detaching myself from my mother. I actually told her many times that, unless she left him, I would teach myself not to love her.

Then, I had the painful memory of my hospital stay in the children's ward. Whenever the children would get together to play tea party, a mean girl in the ward always made herself the hostess. She poured the tea despite the fact that the dishes she used were mine. The mean girl insisted that she be the mother whenever we played family. The mean girl was older and much bigger than me, so she always got her way.

I was also hurt that my father visited me only twice during my entire ten-day stay. On top of that, on the Sunday he visited me, he stopped by my bed to say, "hello," and then he began to joke around with all the other children in the ward, especially the mean girl. I asked my mom why he wasn't being my daddy like he was supposed to.

Around the same time I was watching the John Bradshaw series, I saw the movie, The Prince of Tides, starring Nick Nolte and Barbra Streisand. This movie is about a man who must face his own painful memories for the first time while trying to help his ill sister. Watching his agonizing process really upset me. I walked out of the theater feeling numb inside--it hit too close to home.

Every day I could feel the ball in my stomach getting bigger and bigger. Well, if it wasn't going to go away, I figured I would have to get to know it, so I started talking to this imaginary ball. I even struck a bargain with it.

"Imaginary ball," I said, "I know you are getting bigger and bigger because you want to leave. You want to get out. But I won't let you out unless you make a promise to me. If I let you out, you must make me a better person."

I had to face the fact that there were quite a few things I could improve on. I should be more outgoing, more caring towards others, and less reclusive. There was a whole world out there that I was trying to avoid.

By this time, Chuck had built himself quite a reputation, and I was proud of him. The big companies were now chasing after him. He was improving himself by becoming more successful. Others listened to what he had to say, but what about me? Was I going to be left behind--a prisoner of my memories and fears?

One event I really looked forward to was our trip to the Concord Resort in the Catskill Mountains of New York State. This is the type of place where you can eat and eat and not even realize what you are doing to yourself because you're having fun. Usually, I try to discipline myself. However, this year I must have relaxed because by the end of the trip, I had gained four pounds.

When we came home, I had a message from Myrna to call. She sounded cheerful and we made arrangements to go out for dinner on January 3rd. The evening of our dinner, we almost drove right past their house because we didn't recognize the car parked in the driveway.

Barry let us in. When Chuck told him that we had almost passed by because we hadn't recognized the car, Barry said that he had traded his small brown car for a big black car. Chuck congratulated him on his new toy. I handed him the cake we had brought to celebrate his and Myrna's birthdays, both of which occurred in early January. Jarod and Michael hung out with the Kramer's two children, and we all enjoyed a great evening.

After dinner, Barry and Myrna invited us back to their home. Barry opened a bottle of a rare after-dinner liqueur for us. He explained that this was one of only three such bottles in the country. While we were all eating birthday cake in the living room, we settled into watching an episode of "Nightline." The subject of the show was silicone implants. Barry couldn't enjoy the show since he was frequently interrupted by phone calls from his partner, John Reed. As Barry talked in the background, I could hear him laughing. After the program, Barry related to us that he and John had been best friends since elementary school. I told him that was really neat. Before leaving, we made plans to go out again sometime toward the end of the month or even at the beginning of February since that is when Chuck and I celebrate our birthdays.

A week later, Chuck bumped into Barry at the cleaners. They talked about getting together again, and Barry said, "Why don't we let our social secretaries take care of it?" Chuck replied that since we had already invited them out a couple of times, Myrna should give me a call. This was Chuck's way of being sure Myrna really wanted to continue our friendship. After all, she gave me a hard time about making plans in the past. This way, we would know that she enjoyed our company.

Several weeks earlier, Chuck had been invited by one of his business associates to a very elegant Christmas party that takes place each year. The party attracts a number of wealthy people, so Chuck was looking forward to going.

He was really excited as he told me that, in the past, Richard Nixon, Cher, Frankie Valli, and other famous people had shown up. Instead of sharing Chuck's enthusiasm, I was thrilled when it happened that our vacation plan coincided with the party and prevented us from attending. But there would be similar functions in the future with the rich and famous, and the thought nagged at me: What do I have to offer these people? I wondered how I could gain confidence in myself.

One person who might tell me was the Old Lady. So, I closed my eyes and walked right into the shack to see her. I surprised myself because I found that I didn't have to go through the entire ritual of walking over the bridge, through the tropical forest, and around the bend. Today I just walked right in and started to talk to her. Also, I noticed that she now was very easy to talk to. I told her that she was easier to talk to, and she said quickly, "This is because you listen to me." She was right about this. Then, I asked her the big questions that were on my mind.

"Are the rich and famous going to like me, and am I going to do well with them?"

"Yes," she replied.

"Well, if the rich and famous are going to like me and you're the old me, then why do you live in a basic shack in the Caribbean?"

She smiled. "Because that's the ultimate way to be."

I related well to this because, despite our financial success, I have had relatively little interest in material things. From our conversation, I knew that I would eventually fit in with the rich and famous, and once I did, I would have overcome my fear. Then, I would be able to be whatever type of person I wanted to be. I knew, though, that it would be a long time before I would reach this point in my life.

Something else started to bother me. I would be forty-five on the thirtieth of January. I was getting old. This had bothered me in the past, but it was different this year. I was now reaching a point in my life where I wanted to start to turn things around for myself. I had the surgery done so I would look better in a bathing suit, and I exercised so I could feel better about myself. I was also starting to realize that I would be traveling with Chuck more now that my kids were older. At last, I would emerge from the cocoon of my house. This both excited and scared me.

I realized that my body was very frail and knew it could hold me back from doing what I wanted to do. Hadn't I learned that from my debilitating back injury? Also, in the back of my mind was the inescapable fact that I was nearing the age at which my Aunt Florence, my favorite aunt in the world, had died from cancer. Even though I only saw her once a year, I remember how I used to love being with her. I know she loved me very much, too. When she was forty-eight, she was diagnosed with cancer. She never made it to her fifties. Now that I was getting closer to her age, it started to bother me.

A light feeling of sickness was overcoming me. I felt uneasy and a little out of it--like when you are just about to get the flu. Two days before my birthday, I received a card from Myrna. There was a note attached inside the card, saying that we should get together on February 22nd. While I was happy to hear from her, I decided to wait a little bit before calling her. When I finally did call her a couple of weeks later, I was a different person than the one she knew or, in fact, a different person than anyone knew.

I was having trouble sleeping. One night as I was lying on my bed, I got a phone call from my brother Larry. He wished me a happy birthday. Although we had a normal conversation, there was something in his voice that triggered a reaction inside my body. As soon as I got off the phone, I started to feel really sick to my stomach--so sick that I thought I was going to faint. I had never experienced such a quick onset of sickness as I had that night. The ball in my stomach was heavy. It was getting too big. It was starting to explode. All I could do was rest and hope that this unexplainable sickness would go away.

The next day after this episode, Chuck had to leave for Atlanta on a business trip. I was still feeling sick inside, but I told him to go and not worry about me.

Carol was worried that I hadn't called her in several days, so she got in touch with me. I tried pretending that nothing was wrong, but she knew me too well. Usually, when I talk to Carol, I am able to get a better hold on what's bothering me. She got me to talk about how I felt.

She was about to hang up when I began to tell her about an astrology chart that a friend of mine plotted for me when I was in my twenties. Although somewhat skeptical, Carol was fascinated by the science of astrology. And since Carol and I share our birthday, she encouraged me to tell her about my chart.

"Your chart is like a map of your life that is based on the position of the planets at the time you're born," I explained. I told her that the astrologer said I am an Aquarius with a Capricorn rising and that my moon is in Taurus. "'The Age of Aquarius'--remember the song? It says the Age of Aquarius promises sympathy and understanding."

"I could use some understanding, too," replied Carol.

Then I related to Carol the most important information that the astrologer had given me. She had told me that I had a grand trine which is the highest astrological occurrence anyone can have. A trine is where all the planets come together at one place, and it also means that there is something brilliant about that person.

"Carol, someone called me nine days before my birthday to tell me that January 21st is the day that the world went into the Age of Aquarius." Carol's advice was for both of us to prepare for a big change.

After we talked, I couldn't get the chart out of my mind. If it's true that the world went into the Age of Aquarius on my birthday, then was it possible that the changes the world was going through may have caused some of the changes that I was about to go through? Was I about to experience my grand trine?

## Chapter 6

I'm getting smaller and smaller and smaller. They've put me in a hospital, and I'm shrinking. Fluid is seeping out of my right arm. They put a bucket under my hand to catch the fluid. A doctor is hooking up an IV into my left arm.

"Please call my doctor, Barry Kramer. Tell him to hurry." But Barry does not come. I am dying.

They give me three waves of intravenous. Each wave sickens my stomach. I call Barry's house and one of his kids answers the phone. I say, "Tell your dad that Linda Gilman is in the hospital and dying. Tell your dad to please come."

I am facing the door, waiting for Barry to come. He doesn't come. I turn and notice the window. I know I have to go to it so that I can see my whole life pass before me. It is pitch black outside. I open the window. It feels like thirty degrees below zero. It is so cold that my arms, my legs, and my face freeze. I stand there as long as I can. I stand there until I can't look any longer. Then, I go back to my bed and I am saved.

A few minutes later, Barry enters. When he sees my condition, he says, "I never knew you were sick. I never knew you needed me."

I bolted up from my bed. I had just experienced my second psychic dream. Just as my first dream had been very real, so was this one. I could still feel the sensation of being cold. I wondered when these events would start to play out in the real world.

The sickness that had come over me on my birthday was now getting worse and worse. It was so nauseating. It was truly a birthday gift from hell. I couldn't eat and I couldn't sleep. I couldn't even hold a normal conversation with anyone.

When I told Chuck and some of my friends that this was a psychic dream, none of them believed me at first. They all said it was probably just a regular dream and told me that I should ignore it. But I was beginning to feel like I had a power that none of them could possibly comprehend because it came from something higher than people.

Whether I knew it or not, I was beginning to respect my own feelings. I knew that this dream was the method that unknown spirits were using to communicate with me, and I was going to listen.

I was breaking down physically, mentally, and emotionally. I knew that. My friends knew it, and Chuck was beginning to fear what would happen to me. I knew I had to go through the painful process of reliving my past and ridding myself of the torment within me. Even if it killed me, I needed to do it. Mary Ann said that I was having a nervous breakdown. Maybe I was, but the word that came to me when I was finally able to meditate was "catharsis." I looked up "catharsis" in the dictionary. It refers to a cleansing or a purging. To me, it meant an emotional enema.

It felt like a great vomit was spewing out of me, so I had absolutely no room for food. I was crying for hours every day. I was becoming manic while at the same time I felt depressed. I certainly was anorexic. I punished my body. I started to bleed from my intestines. When I had my period, it wouldn't stop. I was scared that I would bleed to death.

I felt like I had an orchestra leader in my head who was conducting a cacophony of agonizing memories. Sounds of my father screaming at us when he got lost on the expressway during a Sunday drive...sounds of kids jeering at me because I was Jewish...sounds of my mother sobbing. Pieces of my life popped in and out of my conscious mind in a crazy Alice-in-Wonderland order.

They only way I could put these images in order was to put myself into a trance and bring myself back to the time period of my childhood. Sometimes, I would just sit down and meditate. Other times, I would dance to the radio for hours on end and spin off into my own world. Then, there were the times I would simply stare at the pattern on my basement rug and walk around in a series of circles until I had hypnotized myself.

Once I was hypnotized, I was able to see myself as a little girl. It was like I had traveled out of my body and gone back to the 1950's. I would hover on the ceiling of the kitchen in our old apartment where I could look down and see the back of my head sitting there at the pink and charcoal kitchen table. I was able to see everything that went on. The turbulence of the household was embedded in my nerves.

Facing my childhood was not something I wanted to do, but it was something I was compelled to do. In my dream, I walked up to the window and stared into my cold, dark past until my body nearly froze.

I used to walk back and forth to school twice a day because they didn't serve lunch in school, and lunch was the main meal for our family. Although it was a distance, I sort of enjoyed the walk. The thing I didn't enjoy was walking in the door and not knowing what to expect. My father and brother were home for lunch also. Whenever my brother left food on his plate at the end of a meal, my father would loosen his belt and beat him with it until my brother would scream. It was horrible. I had to sit there and watch this violence, and then I had to walk back to school and pretend nothing happened. My father would never hit me because of my scar and because I was a little girl.

The first person to believe in my psychic dream was my mother. After I explained the dream to her, I told her that I would need her help getting through this breakdown. I assured her that even though the memories that I would be facing involved the hateful feelings I had towards her when I was a child, I no longer felt angry towards her. I told her I needed her to be my friend.

She said, "Of course, I'm your friend." My mother said this with a firmness she never had before my father died.

The next person to believe in me was Janet. Janet called me every day. She listened to all of my stories and helped me through my problems. Then, my two sons started believing me.

Jarod was not at home to witness what was happening to me, but Michael was. Michael is a giver, and he was the best help I ever could have asked for. He took care of me physically--just like he had when I suffered from my back injury. Michael put himself in charge of running the house. Janet commented that it was no accident that Michael had been born in the end of June. He is a true Cancer; he has nurturing qualities, and he is kind.

Chuck did his part, too. When Mary Ann suggested that he put me into a hospital, Chuck refused. He insisted that those who loved me best could best care for me. Although my husband loves elegant food, he reluctantly picked up Roy Rogers food for the three of us after he finished work each night. For some reason, Roy Rogers chicken was the only food I wanted to eat.

My friend Mary Ann, who is a board-certified psychologist, diagnosed me as "manic, depressive, and anorexic" with psychotic episodes. "I think you need some professional help," she told me, point-blank.

I refused to accept her diagnosis as I continued my own therapy. I was getting much better at projecting myself back into the world of the fifties. Every day, I would come up with a different image of the past. I remembered how I would go to school every day with the same group of kids. We made all four trips to and from school together. Sometimes, we would get rides from the adults we knew. One adult was Mr. Perozy. Mr. Perozy owned a shoe repair shop. The other regular driver was a grandfather who told us he was seventy-nine years old. He said he didn't have much to do, so he did most of the driving.

Unfortunately for me, this grandfather had it in for my father. He said that when he had his dry-cleaning shop, my father never came in. He asked me in front of the other kids why it was that nobody from my family had taken turns driving.

"My mother has a fear of driving," I answered, "and my father can't drive because he can't leave his drug store unattended." This did not satisfy the grandfather who began to take his anger out on me. From the moment I would step into his car, he would verbally berate me for being related to my parents.

One day, I was in the car while it was pouring rain outside. As soon as the grandfather began to abuse me, I got out of the car and slammed the door. I started to walk in the rain. He pulled up along side of me. "Get in--it's raining," he called. I refused. From that day on, I never took a ride from that man again. It didn't matter what the weather was like. It could be rain, sleet, or blizzard. I would walk all by myself while the other kids were getting a ride because I refused to be treated without respect.

It was now a week into February of 1992. To say that I had a lot on my mind would be a gross understatement. Not only was I trying to come to terms with my past, but I had to deal with my present and future, too. I was going through so much at the time that I really didn't know if I was going to have a future. Would this catharsis ever end?

Desperately seeking answers, I went to visit the Old Lady. I walked into her shack. She was seated on the bench as usual. I looked at her for quite a while. "You're the old me, aren't you?" I asked.

"Yes," she answered.

Then I said, "I'm the young you."

Again, she said, "Yes."

Finally, I asked her if I could see what her body looked like. Without hesitating, she showed herself naked to me, and I told her that she was beautiful. I really thought that she looked old and wrinkled, but I loved her too much to tell her that. I continued to ask questions because I was really starting to understand her. "Are you going to be with me when I die?"

"Yes."

Then I asked, "Can you tell me how I am going to die?" She told me she couldn't. "Do you die when I die?"

"No, no," she insisted. "I am the eternal you."

Suddenly, I snapped out of the trance, picked up my head, and saw a light directly in front of me. It was actually a light bulb on the kitchen chandelier, but for a brief moment, I had seen the light that leads to eternity. I knew then that we don't die; we go on eternally. I knew that I had seen my eternal soul. This moment was so intense I had to believe it happened.

Only a few nights later, I experienced another intense moment. I was lying in bed very late at night. Only a sliver of the moon peaked through my window. I looked at the alarm clock. It read four o'clock. Suddenly, a memory of my father flashed before me. I remembered how every time I used to ask him for a favor, he would sarcastically reply, "Sure, I'll do it at four o'clock in the morning." As this memory floated back to me, I became upset inside. I closed my eyes tightly, walked up to the shack, and went inside. But no matter where I looked, I could not see the Old Lady. Now I was even more upset. I started to cry. This was the very first time I had ever walked in and not seen her. I felt like I had lost a best friend.

"Where are you?" I whispered. Hearing nothing, I called out louder. Then, I felt the most unusual sensation. I actually felt something pass through me. It was like a prairie wind that started at my head and whipped all the way down my body and out my feet, all in a matter of a second or two. Was it a spirit? Was it the spirit of the Old Lady that had just passed through me?

The next morning I thanked Chuck for providing a safe place for me. I told him that I thought that explains why I enjoy spending so much of my time in my house. I know I have a safe place I can always return to. My house is my happy home, and I never want to go back to an evil place.

Now the middle of February was approaching. I began to notice that I was starting to drop some serious weight. Not only was I not eating, but I had also established a dancing and exercise routine that consumed seven hours a day. In order for me to exercise for that long of a time, I had to put forth gargantuan strength. Ordinarily, I would have tired after an hour or two. Now I was compelled to keep on going because it allowed me to meditate and to fall into trances. Once I was in my trance, I could look out the window and face my past.

Fast.  Exercise.  Cry and bleed.  I would meditate from the moment I awoke until the moment I fell asleep, if I was lucky enough to fall asleep at all.  My mind was punched into the work clock nineteen hours a day.  During the first four months of my illness, I lost a total of twenty pounds.  I went from 105 pounds to 85 pounds.

Not only did I have to deal with the hatred that lived in my childhood home, but I also had to deal with a hatred-- the one called anti-semitism--that lived in my town.  The other kids sometimes didn't want to play with me just because I was Jewish.  I used to hear people called my father the "money-hungry Jew."  They said he would charge high prices in his drug store.  There were only a few Jewish families in this town of more than twenty thousand people.

Sometimes, my father would be in such a violent mood that my mother would take my brother and me out of the house to walk the streets for hours.  When we met up with people, I would have to smile and pretend that everything was fine when inside I felt sick.  At night, their screaming was so loud that my body would start to shake hard; then I would put my fingers into my ears and hum to drown out the sounds.  However, when I felt that the boiling point had been reached, I would start to scream at the top of my lungs as though I had snapped and was totally out of control.  This scared my father and calmed him down.  These memories were so painful that they destroyed my appetite.

Carol pointed out to me that my rapid weight loss represented the first part of my dream in which I was getting smaller and smaller.  I had to agree, and, although the dream didn't include anything about my mental health, I could tell that something was very wrong with my mind.

Mary Ann was beginning to open her mind to the possibility of my dreams being psychic, but she warned me that I should watch out for Stage Two of a depression where the body begins to shut down. I didn't want to tell her, but I was already in Stage Two.

At one point, I began to think that maybe I should go to see a psychiatrist, but I really didn't want to because I was afraid that a psychiatrist would label me as insane and lock me up in a mental institution. I had to admit that there was at least a slight chance that I had lost my sanity and that maybe I really did belong in a mental institution.

It was Chuck who convinced me not to go. After he described a few of the unappealing things they might to do me such as waking me up early in the morning, putting me on a daily routine, and placing me with a roommate, I decided not to try. Chuck reassured me that he and Michael were there to help me through this. Since I already knew how wonderful they could be and how my friends were willing to stick by me, I decided to stay home in my safe place. Somehow, I would get through this catharsis on my own.

Forty-five years worth of pain and suffering were inside of me, and I wanted it all out. I wasn't going to block a single feeling even though a dear old friend named Ellen warned me not to look out the window. She suggested that I put up a curtain so I couldn't see my life. Other friends advised me to take Prozac, a drug which would block my emotions. I appreciated the advice, but I didn't listen. I knew that no matter what, I had to face my life because this was the only way I could become a better person. I was now starting to catch on to the real reason I had the dream. The dream was actually a set of directions I had to follow in order to break through my fears and become the person that I had always wanted to be.

Maybe it would kill me, but I was following what

seemed to be the most important part of the dream, the part where I faced my entire life. At the same time, I couldn't help wondering when and how the other pieces of the dream would come true. One piece I certainly wasn't looking forward to was the part with the three waves of intravenous that would sicken my stomach. I was sick enough as it was; the last thing I wanted was more pain.

Then, one day in mid-February, the first wave broke. I woke up in the afternoon thinking how strange it was that my life had been divided into two lives with the first half being so horrible and the second half being so wonderful. Before getting out of bed, I threw my arms out to the side and said loudly, "My life is so yin-yang."

All of a sudden I felt something pop in my heart. It was a very strange feeling, probably similar to the jolt that a heart attack victim gets when the doctor is trying to save his or her life. It was like a surge of power being sent to my heart and it stunned me. I got out of bed and ran downstairs to tell Chuck about it. By this time, even Chuck, who was practically a saint, started to get disgusted with me because of my erratic, crazy, and highly emotional behavior. So, when I told him what had just happened to me, he was in no mood to listen.

At that point, I demanded, "You'd better take me seriously, Chuck. I'm a very sick person and, if you don't take me seriously, then you will not be able to go on business trips. Instead, you will be stuck home, taking care of me, or spending lots of time with me in a mental institution!" I turned on my heel and went back upstairs to bed.

I was very upset inside. I did not like to argue with Chuck. I flopped on my bed and started to cry. All of a sudden a wave of sickness overcame me. I felt so nauseous and so sick to my stomach that I could taste my own vomit. I started screaming at the top of my lungs. I was screaming about my pain, and I was screaming about my childhood. I could hear footsteps in the hallway.

Chuck threw open the door and ran to me. He took me into his arms and held me tightly. When he asked me what was wrong, I described the feeling to him. Then, I told him I didn't know if I could live like this anymore. The truth was that I didn't really want to kill myself, but for that brief moment, I thought suicide might be the only solution. It didn't take a genius to figure out that this was the first wave of intravenous.

## Chapter 7

Earlier I thought I might have been going insane because of my crazy behaviors and my rapid, uncontrolled weight loss. It wasn't until I started hearing voices in my head, though, that I thought I was joining the ranks of Joan of Arc and Moses.

First, my brain started to feel different. It was like my brain wasn't there and my head was empty. In its place was a hollow tube through which thoughts would come and go as they pleased. Then, voices started to enter the tube. These voices were actually loud voices that talked in my head just like the voice that told me to get off the highway when we were coming back from Washington. These voices would tell me things I wasn't familiar with, and I didn't understand it at first. They frightened me. The strength of the voices made me shudder. Meanwhile, I feared that these voices meant that I was truly insane. I would wake up screaming for them to leave me alone.

One morning, a voice woke me up with the phrase, "Love and understanding is what all humans crave." Another time, I was awoken to the 23rd Psalm which reads:

The Lord is my shepherd; I shall not want.
He maketh me to lie down in green pastures:
He leadeth me beside the still waters. He
restoreth my soul: he leadeth me in the paths
of righteousness for his name's sake. Yea,
though I walk through the valley of the shadow
of death, I will fear no evil; for thou are
with me; thy rod and thy staff they comfort me.
Thou preparest a table before me in the
presence of mine enemies: thou annointest my
head with oil; my cup runneth over. Surely

goodness and mercy shall follow me all the
days of my life: and I will dwell in the
house of the Lord forever.

Gradually, I relaxed enough to listen to these voices. They weren't just there to wake me up. These were also teaching voices. I would ask questions and the voices would answer me with new and different phrases.

One time I said, "Here I am, a nobody. I came from a dysfunctional family and now I'm going to be with all kinds of fancy people. How am I going to do it?"

A voice in my head echoed, "I'm nobody; I'm everybody." Then the voice would say, "Take a stand and show no fear. Courage is the ability to face one's fears. Giving is the ability to take from one's self. Don't be afraid to go up against something you love or want. Less is more. Silence is golden. You can say or do anything to anyone as long as you do or say it in a nice way and have the courage to carry it out."

All of these phrases made sense to me, and I took them into my heart as lessons to live by. I didn't know if they were coming from the Old Lady who was now a part of me, or whether they were coming from the same spirits who had been guiding me my whole life. Perhaps they were just phrases that I had learned as a child but had blocked until now. But it really didn't matter. All that mattered was that I listen to these voices so that I could become a better person. I didn't even care if these voices in my head meant I was crazy because I already thought I was. I became a prisoner of my own mind.

Whether I was crazy or not, I had already determined that I would get through this catharsis without the help of a mental institution, and I was going to keep my word. Just to satisfy my curiosity, though, I asked out loud, "What are these voices in my head and where is this information coming from?"

A voice answered, "This is a gift to be enjoyed, not to be feared."

Then I asked, "Why am I getting this gift?"

The same voice answered, "Because you broke a legacy."

What is a legacy? I looked up legacy in the dictionary. It means a gift, and it also could mean something from an ancestor. I immediately thought of my father. I had started out in life loving my father very much, but the older I got, the more I became disappointed in him. I saw that he was a mean person to us, and I felt let down. I loved my mother, too, but I couldn't show it because she always sided with my father out of fear.

As for my brother, we didn't get along very well, and we used to fight frequently. I used to love to torture him. He would spend hours lining up little army figures along the floor. Just when he had them all lined up for an imaginary battle, I would come and purposely trip over them, scattering them in every direction. Of course, he would beat me up afterwards, but I had fun doing it.

I basically raised myself. When I became a teenager, I rebelled. Since my father was hard-working, moral, and religious and my mother was overprotective, I would do things that went directly against their values...even things that were often life-threatening. Say I wanted a ride somewhere and my father didn't want to drive me, then I would hitchhike. I really didn't want to have to do these risky behaviors because I loved myself and I wanted to live. So, when I became an adult, I decided that I wanted my kids to have a normal childhood so that they wouldn't have to feel the way I did.

The only way I knew how to do that was by doing the exact opposite of what was done to me. Because I was punished for not eating everything on my plate, I would allow my kids to eat as little as they wanted. While I was never allowed to disagree with my father, I encouraged my own kids to always voice their true opinions.

No, I am not a perfect mother, but at least I knew not to follow my parents' example. I made sure that my kids had the self-esteem they needed to make it on their own. At the same time, they knew I was always there for them. I raised my kids right, and for the first time, I started to feel deserving of this psychic gift I was receiving. I had earned it not just because I broke the legacy, but I earned it because I always made sure to listen to the voice when it spoke to me--no matter how it chose to get its message across. Just as a child instinctively listens to its mother because it knows that the mother is only there to help, I listened to this gift because I knew it was there to help me. In fact, this is one of the reasons I believed I had to get through my catharsis. The gift was already helping me. As painful as it was to go through, I knew that I was finally beginning to grieve for my father and to shed all the tears that I had held inside for three whole years. Now I realized why it had happened. I was finally beginning to grieve for my childhood.

Before this whole episode happened, I was someone with two separate and distinct lives. The first twenty-two years were horrible, and the next twenty-three years were beautiful. The second half of my life was now one year longer than the first half, and the scales were tipping. My two lives were coming together to form one person who went through childhood, teenagehood, marriage, children, and a new business. Finally, this person was going to have a future as one complete person. This catharsis was actually a process of integrating two lives into one.

Some of my friends think it is wonderful that I can meditate. The truth is that I first got into the habit of meditating when I was a little girl in school. I didn't like school very much, and whenever the teacher would administer a test, I would rush through it so I could be finished before everyone else. Then, with the spare time I had at the end, I would meditate while doodling on the back of the test. I didn't even realize how much doodling I was doing until one day when the teacher held me after school and hollered at me for scribbling on the test. From that point on, I realized that I enjoyed meditating. It was my way of coping with all the pain I've had to endure in my life.

Not only was I beginning to realize why I was having this catharsis, I was also understanding why it was so important that I get through it on my own. Instead of a real therapist, I would give myself an imaginary psychiatrist. I actually invented a person who could help me get through it. Inventing people is the technique I've always used to make my life a little bit easier. As a child, I had given myself imaginary parents who were kind and loving to me. Then, when I first got married, I gave myself an imaginary bodyguard named Roscoe who had a shaved head. Jokingly, I told Chuck that if he ever did anything to hurt me, Roscoe would get him as they do to a new pretty boy in prison. Chuck never messed with me! Now, during my catharsis, I brought Roscoe back to be my imaginary psychiatrist. I figured that Roscoe would come a lot cheaper than a real one and, with all the problems I was having, he could probably help me just the same. After all, he was already acquainted with me. I felt at ease with

Roscoe. I felt I could tell him anything. I would tell him all my problems, and his response would be the same.

"Hmmm, hmmm, hmmm," he would say. Roscoe turned out to be the best psychiatrist anyone could ever ask for because he didn't read out a long list of psychological labels, and he was always there to listen to me.

After a while, the orchestra leader in my head was beginning to conduct more of the present issues in my life, putting aside more of my childhood memories. My present problems became my primary concern. Was I crazy? Why was I chosen to receive this gift? What was I supposed to do with it? There were other issues I had to face as well. Some were issues that just didn't make any sense to me. Some were issues that upset me very much.

One thing was particularly upsetting to me. It happened only two days after my first wave of suicidal feelings. It was something that I had read about in books, but something which I never knew could actually happen. This strange event was not a dream because I was wide awake when it happened, but I was in a meditative-like trance. I was a very courageous male Indian. I went out to fight a warring tribe. On my way to battle, I came across one of the enemies lying on the ground with an arrow in his shoulder. It was Barry Kramer. I looked into his eyes and, instead of killing him like I was supposed to do, I pulled the bloody arrow out of his shoulder. He got back on his black, brown, and white horse with its red blanket. We both went back to his tribe. When he told his tribe what I had done, they had an incredulous look on their faces. Barry's wife, Myrna, was also there, but all I could see of her were her eyes.

I felt like this was an actual memory from another lifetime because the vision was as vivid and real to me as was my memory of last night's dinner. This vision came to me in three stages and at three different times during my catharsis. This was the first of the three stages.

## Chapter 8

My catharsis was making me absolutely miserable twenty-four hours a day. I needed something to blame for this misery, so I chose the psychic gift, a gift which I hadn't asked for and that scared me out of my wits. If there had been a goal in sight, like my developing the ability to read people's minds, then I might not have minded being temporarily miserable. But there were no goals. There was only the hope that something good would happen to me in the end. It was like I had inherited a multi-million dollar estate--but under one condition. First, I had to learn to get along with my mother-in-law who would be living under the same roof with us. Of course, this would be a lengthy process to learn to live together in peace; and it might nearly kill me, but I would have the hope that someday I would inherit the estate.

I knew this psychic gift was something of great worth, although its worth was measured in terms of what it could do for me and not in terms of money. It gave me a power that others did not possess. After all, hadn't it told me about my father's death one week before it happened? Hadn't it warned me ahead of time about my painful catharsis? I felt there was no telling what it might do for me once it could be properly developed. Maybe that's what my feeling of pregnancy as the ball developed inside of me was all about--it was about giving birth to a gift which was only in its infancy, a gift which would take pain to develop.

My first priority, however, was very basic. I had to get through this illness. The agony and torture up to this point had been almost unbearable. It had nearly killed me. It felt like I was being dragged to hell and back and all for no apparent reason. Unanswerable questions constantly flooded my mind. When would this torture end? Was it ever going to end? Yet, something kept pushing me forward. Something kept me plastered to that window and wouldn't let me quit. That something was the desire to rid myself of all the pain within me. Only then could I become a better person and, eventually, further develop my psychic abilities.

I couldn't help wondering when the second stage of my vision would appear. Maybe if I called Myrna, I would gain more insight into what this vision meant. It was still mid-February, and I had not called her yet to thank her for the birthday card. Nor had I called her to let her know if February 22nd would be okay for dinner. Of course, I really didn't want to call her because I was in the middle of my breakdown, and I was not in a particularly heathy state of mind. Despite my reservations, I kept remembering from the second psychic dream that eventually I was to be saved and that after I was saved, Barry would walk into my room. With this in mind, I became desperate to go out with them on February 22nd. Seeing Barry at this dinner might signify the end of my catharsis.

On February 21st, I was feeling no better. However, I couldn't cancel because I wanted to be saved and I felt this was my big chance. That night, I received a call from Myrna. She called to tell me that they might have to cancel because Barry had the flu. I had two opposing feelings. I was upset for my sake, but I was also relieved that I might not have to go. Myrna called back the next day. First, she cancelled the dinner. Then, she asked me how I was. I decided to clue her in as to what was happening to me. I told her I couldn't eat or sleep and that I was very sick all the time. I think she was surprised to hear this. Finally, she asked how I was coping with this sickness. I told her that I had very bright friends who were there for me whenever I needed them. Before we got off the phone, we rescheduled dinner for Saturday, March 21st.

Before the end of February, the second stage of my past-life memory came back to me. After seeing Barry's tribe, I went back to my own tribe. It was important that I talk to the shaman, the tribal medicine man. I walked into the shaman's teepee.

I couldn't believe my eyes. The shaman was Robert Greenberg! Although the inside of the teepee was dark, I could see Robert dancing and jumping around in front of the fire. All of the Indians were throwing their buffalo skins and other worldly goods in his direction.

While he was dancing, I told him what I had done. I had saved an enemy. I thought he would be mad at me. Instead, he stopped dancing. As I stood there wondering what would happen next, he looked directly into my eyes and then put his hands on my head as if to bless me.

I did not know how to interpret this part of the vision. However, I found it interesting that Robert played a major role in my tribe. This brought up a new issue for me to deal with: why were Robert and Barry, two prominent, well-respected, successful men playing such a big part in my life? Not only had they done so much for me in this lifetime, but it looked like they each had a big part in my past lifetime, too. Barry is a wonderful surgeon who has received many accolades for his work, and Robert has built and operated a billion-dollar company. And here I was--a reclusive housewife from a dysfunctional family. Why was I associated with these two powerhouses? I was beginning to question whether I wanted to be a recluse forever.

One day in the beginning of March, the memory of my father lingered with me throughout the day. In fact, I spent the entire day trying to understand him and trying to figure out if he really did love me even though he managed to make my life a living hell. After thinking and thinking and coming up empty-handed, I decided to call the person who knew him best--my mother.

My mother was glad to hear from me. After I listened to her news, our conversation drifted back to my childhood surgery. This time, I began to recall something very important. I remembered coming home from the hospital and hearing my father cry about my scar. I also remembered his mentioning that he actually did visit me in the hospital more than twice, but I was fast asleep when he came and he didn't want to wake me. As I told this to my mother, she faintly recalled it.

"Was this memory real?" I asked her. I thought it was very possible that my mind had been playing tricks on me throughout this whole mental collapse and that this memory might be just another trick. Besides, it didn't make any sense to me why I would remember this now and not during the time that all the other surgery memories were coming back to me.

My mother and I started to put two and two together. She reminded me how after closing his store at ten o'clock each evening, my father used to drive over to his parents who lived an hour and twenty minutes each way just to drop off some medicine for them. I remembered how one time when my brother went on a camping trip in elementary school, my father drove all the way out to the campsite after work just to drop off another blanket for him so he wouldn't be too cold. Together, my mother and I figured out that he really liked to do nice things--that inside his personality could be a nice person. Since the hospital was less than fifteen minutes away from our house, it made sense that he probably had told the truth when he said he came to visit me more than twice. I confirmed my belief deep-down inside that my father really did care about me.

But what on earth made me remember my surgery from forty years ago? Was this the one missing piece of information that would allow me to understand my father's love for me? I have my own answer. I believe that my father wanted me to remember this surgery. All my life, I hated him because I thought he abandoned me when I was four. Maybe he knew this and he couldn't rest until I had discovered the truth. So, it is possible that he used Barry Kramer as his instrument to deliver this message to me.

By purposely guiding Barry to visit me at the hospital on the night of my adult surgery, could my father have been providing me with the tools that were necessary to dig up the memories of my childhood surgery? Of course, it made me wonder why a stranger would come to visit me when my own father would not. My father must have figured that I would have to face the fact that I had started to lose my love for him when I was four years old. Knowing that my mother would be helpless without him, he figured that we would become closer, and she would help me to see that my father really did visit me while I was asleep. With this new information, I would be able to find it in my heart to forgive him, which I was slowly starting to do.

That night, before falling asleep, I saw colored dots on my ceiling again. The dots came to life and were moving all around. Chuck was away on one of his business trips, and I was all alone and scared. I thought they would never leave, so I hid under the covers and screamed, "Go away, go away, leave me alone!" Magically, they left.

Was this sickness getting to a point where it might kill me? Every single thing I was doing, besides sleeping, was contributing to my weight loss. The only control I kept over my weight was through trying to eat a lot. But whenever I tried to eat, I could only take in a little bit before feeling like I would throw up. I was getting smaller and smaller and smaller and smaller. At one point, I had gotten so small that my rear end was starting to fall through the toilet seat. This is when I became frightened for my life. I used to scream at my family, "Everybody must let me be! Can't you see I'm wasting away to nothing?" This was one issue that was becoming a matter of life or death.

In mid-March, I experienced the third and final stage of my past-life memory. After Robert seemed to bless me in his tent, I walked outside into the sunlight. I walked across an empty field. Some of my tribe were following beside me. At the end of the field was the beginning of the trees. There at the treeline stood Barry. He was on foot. He was holding the rope on his horse. The red-brown feather in his headpiece was pointing down. His hair was worn long and parted down the middle. Some of his tribe stood near him. He was slightly in front of them, making me think he was the son of the chief or someone else very important in that tribe. They stared at me. I was the special one. And, then, Barry and I were friends.

Was I going crazy? Was this a vision from a past life? Was it real? Nobody believed that it was a vision from a past life, and nobody thought for a minute that it was real. I didn't even believe it myself. I thought that my mind was so overloaded with information that it was tumbling all these jumbled-up facts from my life into a fiction story with Robert and Barry as the main characters. But where did all the Indian stuff come from? I was clueless. All I could do was to hope that I hadn't already gone off the deep end. I decided that only time would tell. Maybe the events would play out as they had in my psychic dreams.

It was now March 21st. In my last conversation with Myrna, she had told me that Barry doesn't like to sit through long dinners with just anyone, but he wanted to be with us. I also remember her telling me during one of our previous conversations that they like to have fun when they go out. Would I have to entertain them at dinner? What if my depressive side takes over and cause me to cry? Then what would they think? Although I could be either happy and fun or sad and boring, I could not act normal. At the dinner, I was determined to bring out the manic side of myself. I acted funny, charming, and happy. In fact, I was so unlike the person I was at home that I should have received an Oscar for my performance. As some of my thoughts came out wrong, I even slipped and said some obnoxious things to them in my serious effort to be funny.

During the course of the dinner, Myrna showed me the article that I had asked her to bring when she had mentioned it in our last conversation. The article was written by a family whose nine year old adopted daughter was a patient of Barry. It praised Barry for his compassion and humanity. According to the story, this little girl had been severely burned and abused in other ways by her biological mother. The girl and her mother lived in a foreign country. In order for a medical visa to be issued to allow the girl to be operated upon in the United States, her adopting family had to obtain a commitment from a surgeon promising that he would perform an operation to reconstruct her hands. The article talks about how Barry made that commitment and how he had subsequently performed numerous surgeries on her hands, enabling the little girl to later participate in various sport activities. She recovered enough to participate in a dance recital. The family thanks Barry in the end of the article and tells him how grateful they are to have known him. This article only confirmed what I had already known about Barry. I was proud of Barry, and I wanted a copy of the article for myself.

Later in the dinner, Barry and Myrna noticed that I wasn't eating much, so Chuck explained to them that I was sick. At that point, I decided to tell them why I couldn't eat. I told Barry that I had a bad childhood and that a lot of my memories were coming up to the surface. Barry told me that I was going through a catharsis. I agreed because it confirmed what I already knew. I described some more of my symptoms to him, but I was acting too funny and looking too good, despite my weight loss, for him to realize the full severity of my sickness. In fact, up until the time I told them, which was halfway through the meal, neither Myrna nor Barry even suspected that I was sick. And, when I told them, they still had a hard time believing it because of my upbeat behavior that night. After dinner, we invited them back to our house.

The first thing they wanted to see was our exercise equipment because they were interested in buying some equipment for themselves. After showing them what we had, we all sat down in front of the fireplace. While we were getting comfortable, I began to tell them a story that could be interpreted in several ways. Although I had always thought of it as a psychic event, I was curious to hear how Barry would view it.

Something very lucky happened to us during one of our low-income years in the mid-1980's. Chuck had decided to change the log system in our fireplace from regular wood logs to gas-fired logs. This was an expensive change, and I thought that he was crazy for wanting to spend our money on it. Also, since it was the month of May, we wouldn't be putting these logs to use until late fall or early winter. However, Chuck was in charge of these matters, so we went ahead with the new system. When the men came over to change our logs, they discovered a gas leak in our basement. They said that had we lit a match down there, the whole house would have blown up.

Throughout the story, I kept my eyes on Barry. Afterwards, I asked him if he thought this incident was bizarre. I wanted to hear his reaction to this so I could figure out if he believed in spirit guides or anything higher than people guiding us. Then, by hearing his answer, I would know what his reaction would be later on when I would choose to tell him everything that had happened to me. He simply said, "No."

I wasn't sure if he meant, "No, this kind of stuff happens all the time, but I don't think much of it" or "No, this was definitely a psychic event." I decided that I had said enough, and I did not push the issue any further.

Before they left our house, Barry slapped me on my arm. "Linda, you're such a pisser." This meant a lot to me. Chuck and I gave them some gifts for their two kids from our large collection of product samples. These were expensive gifts that we would not have given to just anyone. We gave them to show how much we liked Barry and Myrna. I forgot to tell them not to bother to send a "thank-you" letter. I also forgot to duplicate the article Myrna had brought to the dinner, although it would have been easy to copy it on Chuck's machine.

For the next couple of days, I was bedridden. I had put forth so much energy in trying to be funny and in trying to squelch my depressed feelings that I was now too weak to move. It was the next week when Chuck got around to calling Myrna to give her the name of a photographer that she needed for her daughter. A couple of days following Chuck's call, Myrna sent me a copy of the article I had wanted along with a note which read, "Had a great time Saturday. Let's do it again, soon." She signed it, "Love, Myrna."

I had to wait about ten days before I felt well enough to call her. When I did call, one of her kids answered and said she wasn't home. When I told Chuck that she hadn't returned the call in several days, he thought that Myrna hadn't gotten the message I had left and suggested that I call her again. When I called back, Myrna answered the phone and told me she was too busy to talk. She said that she couldn't talk the next day either because she was going to a wedding. But she did say that she would call me on the day after that, which happened to be a Monday.

One positive outcome of this sickness was that I was starting to look better. I knew this because people were telling me so. Instead of appearing haggard and worn out from dealing with all of these hurtful feelings, the opposite was happening to me. I was starting to look younger, and I was looking more vital. The only problem was that, although I appeared attractive on the outside, I didn't feel attractive on the inside. I felt very alone inside of myself. No matter what, I didn't care how I looked or what others thought of my appearance because I had too many problems I had to deal with. This is how I felt until one of Chuck's friends and business associates, a man named Marvin, changed my mind.

During this ten-day sick period, Marvin paid us a visit from Los Angeles. Marvin was one of Robert Greenberg's best friends and, for a long time, Marvin had been a vice president of L.A. Gear. When Marvin came over, Chuck let him in. I was a little hesitant to come downstairs. I resented having to put on an act like I was feeling fine when, in reality, I was feeling awful. I forgot about myself for a minute when it came to my mind that Marvin had many problems of his own. Chuck had mentioned that he wasn't with L.A. Gear anymore now that Disney was involved. I thought to myself that a person with a problem as serious as having lost a job would probably be sympathetic to my problems, too. So, I did my hair, dressed myself attractively, and then came downstairs to see him. By this time, I had dropped sixteen pounds, so I weighed approximately ninety pounds.

Marvin smiled at me. "You're a pretty girl and you know it." I couldn't get over that. I knew that I was starting to look different, but I didn't realize that I could hide so much of my inner pain that I actually appeared pretty on the outside. I was especially taken back by the comment because it was from Marvin. Marvin is a handsome man who was used to being surrounded by pretty, young models when he had worked for L.A. Gear. For him to tell me that I was pretty made me feel really good.

We all decided to go out to dinner. Before we left, I confided to Marvin that I was anorexic and that I wouldn't be able to eat much. Surprisingly, he was very understanding of my situation. He said that someone very close to him was anorexic, too. In fact, he suggested that we skip some fancy place and instead just go to a diner. That was fine with us. We went to a local diner and had a wonderful time.

Marvin was listening carefully to my problems. He made me feel like the pain I was going through was not abnormal which is what I needed to know. Maybe I wasn't crazy after all. I was so encouraged that I told him about my past-life memory and Robert's part in it. When I said that Robert was the shaman, Marvin almost fell off his chair.

"You don't understand, Linda. That's exactly how it was working in the company with Robert." He told me that Robert was king of the company and that my vision was completely accurate. This was the first hint that something from my past-life memory was actually happening in this lifetime.

If I never saw Marvin again, I would always remember how patient and kind he was this evening. I felt renewed and fresh. He had been the first stranger to me who had made me feel good about myself during this illness. I am indebted to him.

## Chapter 9

It was the beginning of April and my catharsis was already two months old. I was still losing weight, and I was still facing my past. If I remembered correctly, there were two waves of intravenous yet to come. The day after I called Myrna, Number Two found me.

It was Sunday evening, and I was lying down on my bed. Suddenly, I felt a wave of sickness in my stomach. The pain was so awful and so sharp that I wanted to die. The whole incident lasted about two hours. If Chuck hadn't been there to hold me each second of those two hours, I don't know what I would have done to myself. I couldn't understand why I was getting these horrible pains without so much as a warning. Maybe it was a physical reaction to the bottled-up emotions I held tightly inside. Maybe it happened because I became upset over Myrna's pushing me away. Maybe it was that imaginary ball demanding to get out. Whatever it was, I knew from the dream that I only had one more wave to go. I prayed to God that when it came, I wouldn't do the wrong thing.

The next day was the day Myrna was supposed to call me back. She never did. On Tuesday, my friend Mary Ann, the psychologist, came in from California and stayed at our house for a couple of days. She diagnosed me as manic, depressive, and anorexic with psychotic episodes. I agreed with the first three labels, but not the fourth. I was not psychotic--I was psychic. Someone had told me that neurotics build castles and psychotics live in them. I did not live in a dream world. When I had experienced my dreams, I had bolted up. I had snapped back to reality.

I asked Mary Ann if she would like to go out to dinner with Janet and me since Janet was well-informed about what I was going through. Mary Ann agreed to go. Janet drove over to my house on Thursday, and the three of us went to a local diner.

When we arrived, we asked to be seated at a booth, but the hostess told us that all the booths were filled. This struck me as strange since not once in the last twelve years have I ever been at this diner on a weeknight during which all the booths were filled. The three of us were directed to a table in the dining room.

We were seated and halfway through our dinner when who walks into that dining room but Barry, Myrna, and their two kids. Before she sat down at the next table, Myrna walked over to me. In a nasty tone of voice, she said, "I was going to call you on Monday, but it was too early in the morning--you wouldn't have been up."

I replied, "You can call me anytime in the afternoon or in the evening." I was pleased that I had given her an answer she couldn't get around. But I was wrong. She was up for the challenge.

"I can't call at night because I go to bed early. I'm tired from taking care of my family all day." Since this was a casual encounter and not the finals in a debate tournament, I let it go.

The three of us began to discuss the latest episode of my breakdown. Mary Ann insisted on her diagnosis while Janet stuck up for me. We didn't argue about it, though. Then, we joked about Mary Ann's last husband. As Mary Ann told us stories, we all laughed loudly.

As we were about to leave the restaurant, I picked up my coat. Barry looked up from his table. "You cost me a lot of money," he said. I couldn't help wondering what Barry meant by that crack. I had to walk over to his table. Then, with a smile on his face, he informed me that he had bought a recumbent exercise bike similar to the one I have. He told me proudly that he was pedaling ten miles a day just like I do. I felt I should update him.

"I'm not sick anymore," I told him. I wanted to let him know I was fighting my sickness, and I also wanted to hint that my sickness had been the reason I acted manic when we had last gone out.

"You weren't sick the last time we went out."

I quickly responded, "Yes, I was."

What did Barry mean? I had definitely told him about my sickness during our last dinner. I remember wanting him to know about it because I hoped he would be concerned about me. Then it dawned on me that I must have been acting so charmingly manic at that dinner that he didn't want to believe I was sick. We said a few more things, and, before leaving, I gave Myrna a kiss on the cheek.

"I hope we can get together again soon." I wanted to end things on a nice note.

When I returned home, I began to meditate on the day's events. Immediately, I formed a connection between the episode at the diner and my psychic dream. In the dream, I was dying. I was getting smaller and smaller and smaller. Sure enough, I now weighed only eighty-nine pounds, the smallest I had been since childhood. The intravenous in my left arm represented my need for nourishment as I was unable to eat for so long. Fluid dripped from my arm. It resembled the tears I shed during my catharsis. I also felt the sensation of oozing blood from the dripping arm, similar to the blood I lost during my excessive menstruation and intestinal bleeding..

I had called Barry's house to ask him for help. One of his kids had answered the phone. I figured that he hadn't gotten the message right away because he didn't show up when I needed him. In real life, a very similar situation had just happened. Last weekend when I called Myrna, she told me that her daughter had never given her the message. When I told Barry that I was sick at the March 21st dinner, I wanted him to be concerned for me. Although I know I told him, he never got the message either.

As I was waiting for Barry in my dream, I faced the darkest part of the catharsis. I stood frozen and looked out the window as my life passed before me. In reality, I froze as well, powerless against the raging memories that resurfaced. Compelled to watch, I confronted my past until the memories stop coming. Both in the dream and in real life, I forced myself to endure the trauma of my past.

After I was saved in the dream, Barry finally showed up, saying, "I never knew you were sick." Again, when I started to feel better and could begin to eat and socialize with my friends, Barry shows up at the table next to mine and says, "You weren't sick the last time we went out." As the dream predicted, Barry never understood the seriousness of my condition.

There was one major discrepancy between this part of the dream and real life. By the time Barry came to me in the dream, I was already saved. When he had come to me in real life, I wasn't completely saved, although I was on the way to getting better. Then, I thought about the dream some more. What did being saved really mean? Maybe it didn't actually mean being cured of my sickness as I had originally thought. Maybe being saved was a state of mind in which things couldn't get any worse--they could only get better.

If this was true, then my catharsis was a journey up a high mountain and I had already reached the top. The hardest part had been trying to get there. I had to climb my way through past, present, and future issues, all without a safety rope. A couple of times I nearly fell and died. But eventually I made it. Still, I could not rest at the top. I had to make the complete cycle. Going down the mountain would be less difficult. I could go a little slower, gradually gaining back the strength I had used in going up. For the first time during this entire climb, I would start to be rewarded for my efforts. More facets of my psychic abilities were beginning to emerge.

Now, I did have a message to share with others. I wondered if I could begin relating to the women in the community. Many women in my own community did not like me because I was different. The truth is that I have always had more in common with men than with women. Men have always fascinated me more, and I had been with boys more than girls when I was growing up.

Thank goodness I do have a close circle of female friends who overlook the things about me that are different. My friends don't care that I don't wake up early and fix breakfast. They accept the fact that I don't go out for lunch because I am busy exercising. They also know I'm not very materialistic. Basically, they accept me for my own qualities. To them, I am nice, honest, kind, and full of great advice. Even my eccentricities are interesting to them. Of course, giving good advice has always been a gift of mine, and I felt that my catharsis had sharpened that gift.

Myrna was obviously one woman who didn't care for me. Why didn't she like me? What had I done? I was trying so hard to be her friend. When I told my mother that Myrna hadn't returned my call, she suggested that I was trying too hard to be her friend.

One of the reasons I was trying to be her friend was

that I wanted to help her whole family just as Barry had helped me. I felt compelled to give something back. I had gifts for their kids. Chuck had connections that could have helped her pretty daughter get into a modeling agency. He had contacts that could have meant lots of additional business with prestigious models and increased press coverage for Barry. Of course, Barry was doing well, but he could have reached the top with a little help. I had a past-life memory in which Barry played a major role. Was I being selfish to expect such a close friendship? After all, I had been Barry's patient, and maybe they just weren't comfortable socializing with patients, even if they had agreed to go out with us. Then again, maybe she didn't mind that I had been a patient of her husband--maybe the truth was she just didn't like me. I guess I wasn't her type. I had to admit that because I was very sick I probably acted a little nuts at the March 21st dinner. For all these reasons, I really couldn't blame her for rejecting me...could I? Still, I was hurt, and that's why I needed to know the real reason she had rejected me.

Luckily, I had other friends to distract me. One day I was on the phone with Janet discussing a problem concerning her. While I was trying to think of a possible solution, a word suddenly popped into my mind. The word was "bargain." I had no idea where it came from, but when I repeated the word to Janet, she said, "What a great idea!" In a matter of seconds, she had taken this word and turned it into a solution for herself. "You're right, Linda, I'll make a bargain with myself. You're exactly right."

Then, Janet explained to me that she had always had a problem with making commitments, dating back to when she was a young girl. I made her realize that she could overcome her problem by making bargains with herself.

Although I didn't understand exactly what she was talking about, I was happy for her and amazed with myself at the same time.

"Maybe I do have psychic powers," I said.

Later on in the conversation, Janet asked me a question to test whether or not I really had psychic powers in terms of coming up with words which would point to a solution for a problem or which would clarify a situation. Janet asked me to name her childhood boyfriend, saying that he had been the cause of her problem by not keeping his side of the bargain. I closed my eyes and began to search my mind for a word. I pulled up the name of Stanley. I felt sure I was wrong since it was such an odd name. There was silence. Then, Janet said, "You're right. His name was Stanley. How could you have known?" I told her I was definitely onto something here. But where are the words coming from? "Perhaps they are coming from your spirits," Janet suggested. I said if that were the case, then maybe I could pull up a word that would help me, too.

After we hung up, I thought I would give it a try. First, I would think of something that was upsetting me. That was simple--it was Myrna. Now, I closed my eyes and started to think. "Why didn't Myrna like me?" Suddenly, the word "loathe" came to me. It was if I had pulled the arm of a slot machine in my head and all sorts of words started to spin around until one finally stuck. I ran upstairs to where I kept my dictionary. I looked up "loathe." The definition reads: "to feel great hatred or disgust for." It had worked! I had retrieved a word from my mind that described what Myrna was thinking of me. I couldn't really confirm that she loathed me, but it certainly made sense that she did. She had taken offense to the fact that I slept late. She had acted nasty to me in front of my friends at the diner. She never called me when she said she would. I was so excited about this new skill that I forgot to be offended by the fact that she loathed me rather than simply disliked me.

The idea of this word game was so fascinating to me that I decided to do a word on Barry. I sat down, closed my eyes and asked myself what he thought of me. Suddenly, I got the word "intrigued." Again, I was amazed. This word did seem to fit Barry's feelings for me. I flipped through the dictionary with lightning speed.

"intrench"..."intrepid"..."intricate"...There it was-- "intrigue." Intrigue means "to arouse the interest or curiosity of." Barry was intrigued by me. Now it was beginning to click. At one of our three dinners, Barry had opened a bottle of liquor that was one of only three of its kind in the whole country. The place we went for dinner was very fancy. He had bought the same exercise equipment that I was using, and he had started the same routine that I had been doing. Yes, Barry was intrigued with me.

What were these words and where did they come from? Was this a form of mental telepathy? At this point, I couldn't tell. If this was a form of psychic ability, though, I would have to further test and develop it. After all I had been through, I was more than ready to explore the positive aspects of my psychic potential.

The next day I was ready to begin another round of words. As I made myself a piece of toast, I concentrated on Myrna. Sometimes, I wish my mind could be wiped clean like Chuck's computer screen, but I am the type of person who has to keep recycling a problem until I come up with a clear answer. As the toast popped up, I asked myself why Myrna hadn't sent a thank-you note for all the expensive presents I had given her kids. I had gotten a thank-you note right after I gave her child a gift the first time we went out. The word "ambience" came to me. My dictionary defines ambience as "the environment or pervading atmosphere of a place or situation." I had to think of how ambience related to Myrna's attitude towards me. Then I hit upon it--she was too disgusted with me to write a thank-you note because everything in her immediate environment had been reminding her of me, including Barry's recumbent bike. My gifts and my ideas were becoming a big part of the ambience of her home, and she hated it.

As I sat down to eat my toast, I continued to think about this new psychic gift. What had I done to deserve it? Perhaps I did break a legacy, but what else was so special about me? Wouldn't it have been more logical to give a gift of psychic ability to someone who was outgoing to begin with? Why me?

It had been weeks since I had bumped into the Kramers. I had received no further communication from Myrna, so I decided it was time to show both of the Kramers a side of myself they had not previously seen. I sent them a very cold letter, asking for a copy of the original bill from my surgery. I closed the letter with "sincerely" to indicate that any friendliness I had towards her was now being replaced with cordiality. Perhaps I was more frustrated than angry with her for not letting me help her family, but if this was the game she chose to play, then I was going to play, too.

I sent the letter on Friday, knowing that it would take one to two days for local mail to reach its destination. On the Friday of the following week, I asked myself what Barry and Myrna were thinking after they had received this letter. Two words appeared in my head. On Barry, I got the word "exasperated," which means "irritated excessively or enraged." On Myrna, I got the word "unabashed," which was not defined in my dictionary. I had to ask Chuck. He said it meant "shameless" or "not embarrassed." Based on the meaning of these two words, I concluded that Barry and Myrna had been fighting over me that weekend. Barry was enraged at Myrna for pushing me away, and Myrna felt no shame for what she had done. She had yo-yoed successfully.

What I liked best about these word games was that they seemed to provide me with a direct channel into people's thoughts. Most of the words made perfect sense which was the reason I labeled them as psychic rather than coincidental. I saw these words as a further extension of my psychic powers, building on my two psychic dreams and on my past-life recollection. I never use these words in my speech. In fact, I had to look them up in my dictionary to learn their meanings! Something up there was communicating to me, and it was now doing so through words given one at a time.

Another time, I asked how Barry felt about Myrna's behavior towards me, and the word that came to me was "insidious" which means "spreading or developing or acting inconspicuously but with harmful effect." It was only natural that Barry would be angry at Myrna for not having given me a chance because he had enjoyed spending time with us.

Before the weekend was over, I did one more word on Barry and Myrna. I asked for a word which would describe what they both thought of the fact that I had sent the letter. I got back the word "audacious," which is defined as "having or exhibiting a fearless spirit." They must have been thinking that I was fearless and shameless.

On Monday morning, I was at it again. Now, I got the

word "mellow" on Barry. I interpreted this word to mean that he was able to put aside his anger so that he could properly deal with his patients.

When I started to do these words, Chuck was quite cynical of my claims that these words were coming to me through psychic channels. He argued with me a lot. "Linda, sometimes you ask for an adjective and you get a noun. That doesn't fit." I told him that I didn't care. He brought up the fact that most words have more than one definition and asked me how I knew which definition applied to the person I was doing words on.

"As soon as I call out the word, other people can apply it to the situation immediately," I explained to him.

Chuck countered, "That's because they're trying to apply it. They expect you to give them a word that will help them, so as soon as you give a word, they force the word to apply whether it does or not!"

I argued that even when a person did the words with me for the first time, the person saw how the word applied to the situation without any help from me, and without taking much time to think about it. Chuck refused to accept this explanation. One time he said, "Linda, lately you are spending more time with the dictionary than you are with me." So I told him from now on, he could call me Dictionary Lady.

No matter what Chuck thought, I knew these words were part of my psychic ability. What did I care if the word was an adjective or a noun? And so what if there were five definitions of the word? The right meaning was coming across. Even if I couldn't explain how it was done, I believed in the possibility. I didn't think of it as an exact science. This was a new talent that I felt I would learn more about as time passed. The only part of Chuck's argument that really bothered me was his suggestion that I was trying to make words fit where they didn't. I had to admit that the words might not always be accurate and, most of all, I might not have proof that every word was right. However, it wasn't long before proof revealed itself.

I knew my friends would be there for me. If a friend of mine needs help, I am always there for that person, so I knew my friends would be there for me. Despite my erratic emotional patterns, my friends were listening to me. If they chose to believe me, it was a bonus. But to me, friendship is understanding and not necessarily agreement.

During this entire illness, Carol was wonderful to me. She knew that this was the roughest thing I had ever gone through, and she also knew just how to make this whole experience easier on me. Through humor, she was able to turn my crying into laughter. She lifted my spirits when they were down. One time, Carol and I were talking about plane crashes. I said that if anyone close to me were to die in a plane crash, I would probably have a psychic dream about it beforehand. She said sarcastically, "If that happens, please give me the ticket. I know a few people I'd love to send on a free vacation!" During another conversation, Carol suggested a little trick we could play on Barry. She told me to take some crayons and draw a picture of him on construction paper as an Indian with an arrow sticking out of his shoulder. Carol offered to make an appointment at Barry's office. When Barry would ask her who referred her to him, Carol would slip out this picture and say, "My friend who knew you seven hundred years ago."

We used to joke around a lot because some of my experiences seemed so ridiculous. But as ridiculous as they were, they were also very real. I wasn't imagining them.

Carol had a hard time understanding my perception. I was able to see her point of view because I realized that she had never had any psychic experiences herself. Since Carol had nothing in her life similar to what I was experiencing, it was very difficult for her to listen to me. I showed respect for her opinions and tried not to overload her with too many of my ordeals. I would have liked to have told her everything, though, because it was Carol who I wanted to believe in me more than anyone else.

But it was my mother who had no trouble believing me at all. Since her mother had been a psychic, my mother was already inclined toward believing my experiences.

My mother was absolutely comforting to me during this time, and I can't say enough about how our relationship blossomed after my father passed away.

Mary Ann, like Carol, had a hard time believing my experiences. Despite all of her professional psychological training, she had never been taught much about parapsychology, and so she was not disposed to believing in psychic phenomena. However, Mary Ann was very supportive of me. She helped me as much as she could despite her busy schedule.

Another person who really went out of her way for me was my sister-in-law Fleurette. Fleurette and I are different. She is very talented in painting and is very interested in all of the arts. She is also very outgoing, and her house is always overflowing with people and parties. But our difference in personality doesn't matter. She took the time to listen to all of my experiences and accepted whatever I had to say to her. In fact, she was one of the first to encourage me to write this book.

Janet believed in me right from the start. She'd had some psychic experiences of her own, and she found mine to be fascinating. One of the qualities I really love about Janet is her positive attitude towards life. She's not afraid to face things. She would always say encouraging things about my psychic abilities. She would tell me not to fear these abilities because they were there to help me, not hurt me. I couldn't have asked more from a friend.

One person who was easy to talk to about my experiences was Ellen. Ellen had known me since we were in our early twenties, so she was my expert in dealing with the first half of my life. One of the things Ellen remembered was how much my scar had always bothered me. Her support for me made me want to help her with her problems. One of her problems was that she had been a heavy smoker for a long time, and now she had gotten to the point where she really wanted to quit. She told me how much she wanted to quit and how it had been so hard for her to do it. I taught Ellen one of the tricks I have always used to overcome any challenge in my life. I told her to create a vision in her mind of a walkway leading to two doors. On one of the doors is a sign reading "Winner." The other door has a sign reading "Loser." The Loser door is much more inviting to enter than the Winner door. When you first walk into the Loser door, it is warm and bright and friendly. Voices are telling you to come in and relax for a while. Behind the Winner door, though, it is cold and dark and very scary. Once you walk through the Winner door, it closes behind you, and you can't leave. But you start to notice that the longer you stay, the warmer, brighter, and less scary it becomes. If you choose the Loser door, it only gets colder, darker, and scarier. "Ellen, this vision can be applied to every challenge you face in life." The next time she called me, she announced that she had been able to quit smoking for good.

I was grateful that I recently had renewed our friendship with Pam and Lew. We had stopped being close with each other for two years. Then, in the spring of 1992, I decided to give Pam a call. I told her how sick I'd been. Pam unquestionably agreed that we could pick up our friendship where we left off. She wanted to put the past hurts aside and be there to help me. Both Pam and Lew took me back into their hearts.

Pam shared with me the experience she had in her twenties in which she felt her mother pass through her. Even though she was aware her mother had died, one evening while Pam was in bed, she felt a presence. An energy field passed through Pam's body, and she instinctively knew it was her mother's spirit. I thanked Pam for telling me this, saying it was a clue to me that my similar experience wasn't so crazy.

Because Pam and Lew were open-minded to everything I had to say, Chuck seemed a little bit more inclined to believe in what I was saying. Chuck always had a great deal of respect for them--the kind of respect that comes from one hard worker to another. He knew how hard Pam worked as the State Clinical Supervisor for Speech Pathology for Skilled Nursing Facilities. He admired how Lew went from being a well-respected rabbi to becoming a well-respected attorney. Later, Chuck told me that if Pam and Lew could be open-minded to my experiences, maybe he could be, too.

It wasn't long before Chuck and I started going out to dinner with Pam and Lew again. Since I was in a highly emotional stage of my life, there were times I just couldn't keep my emotions from seeping out. Sometimes, I would start to cry right at the dinner table. But instead of embarrassing everybody, including myself, I would get up from the table and walk outside to where I could cry alone.

At one of our dinners, Pam told me that I didn't have to leave the table. She said that I could cry right in front of them. She called it, "endearing," to show my emotions in her presence. Pam had a wonderful way of making me feel comfortable in uncomfortable situations. "Afterall, Linda, it won't stop us from eating." I noticed that they never missed a forkful.

Lew also had a way with me. Having once been a rabbi, Lew is very eloquent, and he has always been able to affect me with his words. One time, I asked Lew if he could help me with an issue that was really bothering me. He nodded. I asked him why everybody thought I'm so strange and different.

"I have two popular kids, a wonderful husband, a prosperous business, and a beautiful house," I told him. "Lew, what is so different about me?"

Lew showed me his thumb and forefinger and stretched them apart. He said, "In between my thumb and my forefinger is the norm." Then he asked me to count the number of things in my life that fit into this norm. "How about your marriage, does that fit in the norm? And your kids, do they fit in the norm? And what about the fact that you look so young for your age, does that fit in the norm? And the fact that you don't cook, does that fit in the norm?"

"Lew, you're absolutely right. Most of the things about me are either above the norm or below the norm, but there are very few things that fit within the norm." I took a deep breath as if a huge weight had been lifted from me. What Lew made me realize is that I am different, but that it's okay.

Now, if I could get through this catharsis, I'd be a better and stronger me.

Chapter 10

For the latter part of April and the entire month of May, I concentrated on trying to heal myself. I had already overcome some of the issues that had been pressing me; I accepted that I am different, and I forgave my father. However, several issues painfully remained. I was still losing weight and I was still very emotional, so my catharsis was not yet over.

As confident as I was that I was on my way to getting better, that's how afraid Chuck was that I would remain an emotional wreck forever. Maybe he was becoming shell-shocked over my many outbursts. During the second week in May, Chuck increased his exercise routine in an effort to emotionally escape, but he pushed it a little too far and pulled his back out. I helped bring him upstairs to our bed, and as he was lying there in frustration and pain, he voiced his true feelings about what I was going through.

"We are two different religions. My religion stops at the five senses while yours, Linda, soars into the psychic world. I love you so much, and I am afraid that this catharsis will pull us apart."

I kept reassuring him that it wouldn't. I told him that I would love him forever, regardless of the fact that I probably am from a different world. We laughed about that, and for the next few months, I nicknamed him Mortal Man. The truth is that I love Chuck more than I love any other person on this planet, and I would not let this breakdown or my psychic powers stand in the way of our marriage.

Not only did I have to protect our marriage during this time, but I was also forced to protect my own life. Ever since moving into our house in 1980, we have been bothered by an event that happens from April through July. During these months, our house gets attacked on a daily basis by some very annoying woodpeckers. The birds appear around six-thirty a.m. They peck so vigorously at our house that it sounds like a giant power drill. When it gets to the point where we can hardly stand it, we chase them away. But at nine, they come back and peck some more. They peck again at ten and again at eleven. This usually lasts the entire four months, after which we hear the drilling in our heads.

We have formed our elaborate defenses. In order to scare them off, I coax Chuck out of our bed to go outside and throw things at them. We slam doors and even turn on our extra-loud alarm system. Chuck chases them repeatedly. They always come back the next morning. When Chuck is away on business, which is quite often, it becomes my job to chase away the birds.

This particular year, I was in no shape to be chasing woodpeckers. I couldn't sleep, except for a few early morning hours. I was dropping weight, and I was very sick. Maybe I should pack up and live somewhere else during woodpecker season. Of course, the woodpeckers showed up right on time. They launched right into their endless drilling. But, after two days, they stopped. They left suddenly and did not reappear. I never saw or heard from them again for that year. For the first time in twelve years, the pecking had stopped during the first week.

We couldn't believe it. Why had they stopped coming the very year that a lack of sleep was threatening my life, and I desperately needed them to stop? As I was meditating on this, I remembered having heard somewhere that animals can see spirits. If so, perhaps my spirits had chased them away.

Toward the end of May, Chuck and I were making plans for a combination business and pleasure trip to Chicago and Los Angeles in August. Normally, I don't go on business trips with Chuck, but this time I felt it would be good to just get out of the house and away from my misery. Besides, I always loved to visit L.A., despite the fact that I never wanted to live there.

As we made plans for our visit to L.A., we decided to call Robert Greenberg to tell him that we would both be in L.A. While Chuck had seen Robert fairly regularly, I had not seen him in five years.

"Wait, Chuck," I said, "it would be fun to do a word on Robert Greenberg before we call him." Chuck agreed to wait. I asked myself how Robert was doing and I got the word "pontificate." Since I wasn't familiar with this word, I asked Chuck how to spell it so I could look it up. Pontificate is defined as "to perform the offices of a pontiff (the Pope) or to act or speak pompously or dogmatically."

I had always remembered Robert as very confident and assertive, and he seemed to fit the second part of the definition quite nicely. Then, when Chuck called him, Robert mentioned that he was going to Italy, the home of the Pope himself, in July. I was amazed nonetheless. Robert also surprised me by inviting us to his twenty-fifth wedding anniversary on a yacht in Marina Del Ray. The celebration would take place during the week we had planned to visit L.A. Before the conversation ended, Robert said we could come by his house anytime we wanted.

It was now the end of May, and I had a hunch that my

catharsis was coming to an end. My illness was nearly four months old, and the number four has always accompanied significant events in my life. Shortly after my adult surgery, the number four had served as a catalyst in bringing back memories of the surgery I had undergone at the age of four. These memories touched off a string of traumas which had all combined to form the imaginary ball in my stomach. The ball had exploded, setting off my collapse. Since the 31st of May would be the very last day of the fourth month of my catharsis, I then would be able to find out if my theory was true.

Chuck and I had been invited to the engagement party of his sister's daughter, Lisette. Before leaving for the party the day of May 31st, I put on clothes that made me look very pretty. I also slipped a picture of my father as a teenager into my purse. He is very handsome in this picture. He looks like a movie star--like a young Tony Curtis. The picture would allow me to show others what a handsome man he was. It was something positive I would be able to share about my father. The party turned out to be fun. I socialized, and, as I met people who seemed interested in me, I took out my father's picture for them to admire.

When we got home from the party, I went down to the basement. I turned on the music and started to dance myself into a trance. In this way, I was able to reflect on the events of the day. While in this peaceful state, I was loudly awoken by a presence in the room. It was just there. I wasn't frightened. I sensed it was a man and, then, as the presence grew stronger, I realized it was my father. He was hovering over the old white porcelain scale in the corner of the basement.

I was very calm. When I was sure it was my father, I

said to him, "Daddy, look at me, look how pretty I am now. I've lost twenty pounds." There was a mirror on the scale, and I often looked in that mirror to check on how I was looking in my body suit. Now my father was able to see how pretty I looked--just like he used to see me when I was young and still living at home. As I remembered how he had looked at me, how his eyes shone with pride, I suddenly screamed, "Daddy, I forgive you. Go to the light, Daddy, go. You're forgiven and you can pass on now." In a flash, his presence was gone.

I glanced at the clock. It was six p.m. My father passed on to the next level at six p.m., May 31, 1992.

I fell down to the ground and began to wail. Chuck and the boys rushed down to see what was wrong. I explained every detail of what had just happened. They looked at me wide-eyed. They thought I had flipped. That was okay. Let them think what they wanted. I knew that what I had just felt was real. After three years of holding in my feelings, my father finally gave me the chance to forgive him, and now he could find his peace.

I told Chuck and the boys that I would discuss this later. I had to have the chance to reflect. For the moment, I was content that I now knew my father had heard me when I spoke to him in the hospital a couple of hours after his death. I wondered how many people actually get a second chance to say what they feel to a loved one after that loved one has died. Then, I remembered the story Pam told me about her feeling her mother's presence, and I began to compare our two experiences.

In thinking over what I had experienced, I thought that maybe this was too much for my family to handle. After all, they had been through a lot of pain themselves in helping me to get through my illness. In the end, though, I decided it wouldn't be such a bad idea to involve them in some of the craziness that was inhabiting my mind instead of shunning them just because they didn't believe in my experiences.

Later that night, we all sat around the fireplace discussing this latest occurrence. I asked all of them if they thought I was becoming a different person because of my new psychic skills. My creative one, Jarod, was the first to respond.

"Mom, you've always been different. Now...[he paused] you're just a little more different." I had to smile. Then, we got into a discussion on how I would develop as a person from this point on. It was Jarod who introduced me to a concept which I have found to be very helpful.

This concept was devised by a psychologist named Abraham Maslow. Jarod explained that Maslow's theory of a Hierarchy of Motivation is based on the principle that humans need to satisfy basic needs before addressing more complex ones. The desire to meet these needs motivates us to do the things we do. As we satisfy each need, we progress onto the next level. Maslow recognizes five levels and ranks them by the order in which they must be satisfied.

The first level is physiological needs, or those basic life needs such as hunger and thirst. Although my sickness robbed me of my desire to eat, my needs were satisfied enough to survive. Level two refers to safety and security needs. Chuck and the boys insured my safety and security even throughout my catharsis, so this level was accomplished. The needs of belongingness and love make up the third need. I placed myself at this stage due to my overriding need to be accepted, especially among the people I admired. Once I would begin to feel comfortable around them, I could feel more comfortable with myself, and then I will have entered level four--the self-esteem level. I wondered whether I would ever reach the final stage, self-actualization, when all of my fears and earlier challenges would be met, and I could devote myself to developing all of my potential. I figured that it was at this fifth level when I would be like the Old Lady, filled with wisdom and removed from the materialistic values that all humans possess. Maybe I would find my own shack in the Caribbean.

My son Michael also had a message for me. He recited to me a quote from the Athenian philosopher Socrates: "A life not worth examining is a life not worth living." This quote made me realize just how worthwhile my life really is. It also made me aware of the importance of surviving this breakdown. I was relieved that I had followed my instinct and had invited my sons to share in my problems. Their counsel had enabled me to reach a better understanding of what my life was all about.

I was never a reader, but now I bought all the books I thought looked interesting on the subject of life after death. I especially favored those books which talked about a spirit having unfinished business, hanging around to deliver cryptic messages. The more I read, the more I believed that in order for my father to obtain my forgiveness, he had to eliminate one of the roots of my hatred towards him. The cryptic message he used to help me to understand his love for me was Barry Kramer's impromptu visit on the night of my adult surgery. Through this visit, I eventually discovered that my father really did visit me in the hospital when I was four. The event that triggered his recent visit was the engagement party for my niece where I was showing his picture. This symbolized that I was ready to forgive him.

The next day, things were pretty much back to normal. I returned to my routine of marathon exercising and meditating that I had done every day for the last four months. It was true that my catharsis was not over like I imagined it would be, but my grip on life was getting a little bit tighter. Since May, I had been pulling up words on a daily basis, dating to the day that I had sent the cold letter to the Kramers.

When Chuck saw that I was frequently using my new ability to find out what the Kramers were thinking about me, he jokingly called it, "psychic snooping." On June 1st, I pulled up the word "respondent" on Myrna. This word caught my interest because it means "answering" or "responsive" and I knew it was her turn to respond to my letter. Since it had been three weeks without a response from Myrna, I had figured I would never hear from her. But I was wrong. On the very next day, I got an envelope in the mail from Myrna that was postmarked "June 1, 1992." Although the Dictionary Lady had received the word "respondent," I was stunned. I couldn't believe that this word proved to be so accurate.

For the first time, I actually had documented proof that a word of mine had accurately described what someone else had been thinking. In that envelope from Myrna was a copy of the medical bill and a note, saying we should get together soon. The note was written in a cold style which matched my own. I called her that night because I wanted to clear things up. One of her kids answered and said she wasn't home.

I decided to do another word on Barry. I hadn't spoken to him in quite some time, and I often wondered how his practice was doing. To satisfy my curiosity, I tapped into my psychic world. I knew that one of the reasons for Barry's successful practice was his great relationship with his partner, John Reed. When I asked myself how Barry and his partner were getting along, I got the word "archenemy." This struck me as strange since they had been best friends since childhood, and Barry never indicated that anything was wrong with their apparently "made-in-heaven" partnership. To strengthen my credibility in case the word was accurate, I made sure to write the word down on paper, date it, and I told Chuck about it.

I continued to do words on Myrna. All of the words that came to me centered around the fact that she didn't like me. However, on Friday, I got the word "reconstructional" on Myrna. Maybe this meant that she would be calling to reconstruct the friendship. It had been two weeks since I called her, and she still had not called back.

That night while I was dancing in the basement, the phone rang. Intuitively, I knew it was Myrna. I answered the phone out of breath. I continued to talk to her, trying not to make it appear that I didn't want to talk. Myrna told me that she has been very busy and that was why she hadn't called. Then, she cited the fact that Barry and his partner had recently broken up their partnership as one of the reasons for her busy schedule.

I didn't know quite how to react. Inside, my nerves were jumping around. Not only was I correct about the words "respondent" and "reconstructional," but now I could say that I knew about the break in their partnership before being told about it. Three of my words proved to be right so far. This further reinforced my belief in this strange new gift.

Not wanting Myrna to know that I was already aware of

the dissolved partnership, I acted surprised and concerned. I also refrained from telling her about any of my psychic experiences which involved them, figuring that she probably would not be comfortable hearing about them. Maybe I would tell her eventually, but at this point, I just couldn't expect her, or anyone else for that matter, to react rationally to such a claim.

To change the topic, I started talking about our business. I told her that Chuck and I were going to California at the end of the summer.

"Being with the rich and famous out there will be a real challenge for me," I told Myrna. Then, I described to her the incredible opportunities in New York that we could obtain for her family. I offered to take the pictures of her daughter, who aspired to be a model, and, using Chuck's connections, show them to a top modeling agency. I thought that possibly I could get some of the models to become Barry's patients. I even suggested the possibility of entering Barry into the info-mercial business through Chuck's connections.

"The association of Barry's name with famous models would be incredible for your husband's reputation. Think of the wonderful press coverage this would bring." I let Myrna know that this was reason I had called her, to invite them to dinner with us and some of our connections in New York, but I had put everything on hold since she hadn't called back.

Without hesitation, Myrna declared, "We'll join you." I thought she would have said that she would love this opportunity, and we would love to join you. But, the way she said it, it seemed as if she was doing us a big favor by keeping us company in New York. If I wanted company, I had Chuck. This was something I was doing for them as a favor--something that we usually get paid for doing--and not the other way around. I clarified the situation by telling her that I believed that Chuck and I were fated to help them. Maybe we would change their destiny. As the conversation continued, Myrna said that she would leave the psychic talk to me.

I told Myrna that I weighed only eighty-six pounds. I said it calmly. I did not mention how sick I was. Then, she said something very flattering and completely unexpected.

"You have everything," she told me. I was a little taken aback by this comment because she had never said anything like that before. Although I didn't ask her what she meant, I interpreted her remark to mean that she saw me as having everything I wanted in life. In one way, she was right. On the outside, I did have everything I wanted in life. However, Myrna didn't know about the sickness and the pain I was feeling on the inside. I couldn't tell her how sick I was because I didn't want to use them. Barry was a surgeon, not a psychiatrist, and I didn't want to base our friendship on my emotional needs. Maybe I would tell them on the way to New York. It was such a weird story, though. How could I tell them without convincing them that I was nuts?

Before the conversation ended, we made plans to get together again in a couple of weeks. Since I told her about our extended trip to California, Myrna suggested June 27th. When I told her that June 27th is Michael's birthday, she said we should get together the next evening. However, since Michael's birthday fell on a Saturday, I knew he would want to spend Saturday night with his friends.

"Myrna, it's all right. Let's keep it for Saturday. We'll go ahead and celebrate Michael's birthday on Sunday." Soon after we settled on the date, we hung up.

I couldn't wait to tell Chuck how three of my words had been proven correct. "Now you won't be joking about the Dictionary Lady because she really knows her stuff!" I bragged. For the first time, Chuck was ready to become a believer. I had proof that the words worked!


## Chapter 11


I was still sick. My weight was now down to eighty-five and a half pounds. This is the lowest it had been since I was a kid. I was still grieving over my father. But, the biggest issue I faced was the fact that my life was now multi-dimensional. It included the now which was 1992, the past which involved an Indian tribe existing about 700 years ago, and the reconciliation of the now and the past. The reconciliation was the hardest part of all to deal with. How did this past life fit into 1992? Why were Barry and Robert such important people in both of my lives? All of this was very hard to accept. I remembered hearing a saying that God only gives a person as much as he can handle, but I felt that now God was surely testing my limits.

One night, Chuck and I were at a local diner when we ran into one of Chuck's former business associates. For some reason, this woman, who was crazy about Chuck, acted coldly towards me. But we ended up eating dinner with her anyway. She seemed to be looking down on me the entire time.

The next day, I pulled up a word on what she thought of me. I got "insipidous," which is not in the dictionary, so I checked out the word "insipid." "Insipid" means "without distinctive, interesting or attractive qualities." Excitedly, I ran into Chuck's office to tell him about the word and how it related to last night's situation. I told him that this woman must not have found my qualities to be attractive to act the way she did. Upon hearing this, Chuck automatically shifted into denial mode. He argued that I shouldn't get excited because "insipidous" is not a word. I argued back that it was just a question of semantics, and he was missing the point. The dispute continued with neither of us giving in.

Then, suddenly, all of my emotions came crashing down on me. It was as if all the issues that had recently been building up inside of me seemed to be taking over my mind and my body. For the third time, I felt a sickening wave of pain in my stomach.

All I wanted to do was die. Chuck carried me into our room and placed me on the bed where I screamed and cried over how I couldn't handle my life. I yelled that I wanted to be dead.

The next morning, I found myself lying in bed. I was fully awake since I had not been able to sleep. As the afternoon approached, I finally entered into a half-awake, half-asleep state of consciousness. Once in this state, I started to feel as though I was leaving my body. I came out of my head, went down my body, and then into my stomach. It struck me as strange since my stomach was the same place where I awoke after my adult surgery.

As this was happening, I saw a vision in my head of a bearded figure on the big-screen TV. His hair and beard were long and brown. My eyes were closed during this vision. Even though I am Jewish and I don't believe in Jesus as our saviour, I thought the face looked just like his. At the same time I was seeing him, I heard a very loud and distinct voice in my head asking, "Do you want to go to the next realm?"

Without a second of hesitation, I screamed out, "No!" as loud as I possibly could. I used all the strength left in me to travel back up into my head and open my left eye. Then, I awoke.

As tired and worn out as I was right after this happened, I felt more alive than I had ever felt before. I truly believe that I saw Jesus. Carefully, I made my way downstairs and told Chuck how I had almost died. He looked at me in disbelief.

"What do you mean, you almost died?" he asked incredulously. I explained to him everything that had just happened. While I was talking, I was still shaking.

"Chuck, I could have easily passed on to the next realm. You would have come upstairs later and found my dead body on the bed. Everyone would say, 'That poor woman-- she was only forty-five years old. She was already down to eighty-five pounds, and she was just wasting away. She must have had a heart attack. The stress must have been too much for her tiny body.'" Chuck didn't know what to say. I guess that I had expected too much of Chuck. After all, how could he really understand such strange occurrences when he wasn't experiencing them? I told Chuck that the worst part would be that I would have endured this entire catharsis just to die at the very end. However, I knew from the 23rd Psalm which had woken me one morning, had I chosen to die, I would have made it to heaven.

Later, I called Janet to see what she would say. I told her that there were a couple of very important lessons I had learned from this incident. First, I realized that I was really scared of dying. I never thought that I would fear death, only that I would fear the pain involved in dying. However, when the time to die came upon me, I was literally scared out of my mind. The other thing I learned was never to talk about wanting to die again, no matter how bad things seemed in the future. Nothing could be so bad that I should give up the rest of my life just to avoid some temporary pain. Perhaps, in almost dying, I had acquired a new zest for living.

What do you do on a day you almost died? I did the same things I would normally do--exercise, talk to friends, and try to eat. Only now, I seemed to do everything with more thought and greater appreciation for life. This was my journey, and I could choose the path on which I preferred to travel.

Later that day, Jarod confirmed something I already knew regarding near-death experiences. In a course Jarod had taken entitled, "Death and Dying," he learned that many people who have had near-death experiences have seen spirits and have heard voices just like I did.

That night, I had a very significant dream. I had to go back to school, but I went to the synagogue. It was a Jewish holiday, and my friend Lew was the rabbi who was officiating at the service. After the service, I went home. The next day, I went back to school. I had trouble in my science class and also in my math class. I had no trouble in my English class. I did fine in my history class, too.

I had interpreted this dream to mean that I had a religious and spiritual experience during this breakdown that defied both logic and science, although it had increased my vocabulary and filled me in on the history of myself. The part about having to go back to school represented my need to re-focus on reality. During my illness, I had a hard time focusing on anything but myself. Now, I had to get back into the mainstream of life and start to pay attention to things that were going on around me, including all my responsibilities to my family and friends. I would also have to start putting into practice some of the lessons I was learning, such as having courage and showing no fear.

On June 26th, the day before we were to go to dinner with Barry and Myrna, I called Myrna to verify our plans. She was on a long-distance call, so we quickly made plans to meet a her house at 7:40 and then go to a Japanese restaurant. The next day, Chuck and I got ready early because we wanted to stop by the liquor store to get a bottle of wine for dinner. Just before we left the house, we got a call from Myrna. She said she might not be able to go because her son had been stung by a bee and Barry had some emergencies in the hospital that required his attention. Even though we were all dressed and eager to go, I said, "That's okay. Just take your time, and Chuck and I will grab a snack." I told her to call back when she knew for sure whether she could go.

In the meantime, Chuck and I grabbed a snack. While we were eating, I decided to do a word on Myrna. "How is Myrna feeling?" I asked. I got the word "reconnaissance," which means "the act of reconnoitering or inspecting, observing or surveying an enemy's position, strength, etc. in order to gather information for military purposes." I was blown away because I knew from this word that the past-life memory was real. Myrna and I were from warring tribes. She was checking out my strength because, to her, I was the enemy.

Myrna had a reputation in the area as being one tough lady. As I suspected, when Myrna called back a little later, she said she was definitely going to have to cancel because Barry was still at the hospital, and she hadn't given her daughter dinner yet. Also, she would have to make sure that Barry had dinner when he came home. She didn't mention her son's bee sting.

Her excuse was a tremendous insult. I felt she should have already planned a dinner for her daughter since she knew that she would be going out with us. Also, I couldn't understand why she would have to make dinner for Barry if they were supposed to be going out for dinner. I figured that had I been somebody with whom she really wanted to be friendly, she would have made other arrangements right away for us to get together for a different night. But, she didn't. Instead, she said that she would have to get out her calendar and call me the next day to reschedule for dinner. She asked what time I would be getting up. Because I had gotten the word, "reconnaissance," I knew she was just testing my strength and that she was not going to call back the next day. I told her I wouldn't be home because I was planning to go to the swim club and then out to dinner with some friends to celebrate Michael's birthday.

Not surprisingly, Myrna never called me again. It was over, and I knew not to hold my breath in anticipation of her call. As hurt as I was, there was nothing I could do. She simply didn't want our friendship, and this was something I would just have to accept. However, I didn't have to be sporty about it.

I would keep doing words on them. I figured that they still had to be thinking about me, so I would listen. I asked what Barry was thinking of me. I got the word "auspicious," which means "promising success." I remembered telling him that I wanted to enter Chuck's world and to be with the rich and famous, and I assumed from the word "auspicious" that Barry thought I would be successful. It was at this point that I realized that Barry had a high opinion of me since every word I had ever pulled on him was positive. Another time, I got the word "mercurial" in response to the same question. Two significant definitions of "mercurial" are: "active or lively" and "changeable or fickle." Barry probably thought that my personality was both lively and fickle, and this is definitely how I am. I am always active, and I love to exercise. I am quite lively, and my moods are always changing. When I asked how Barry reacted to the way Myrna had treated Chuck and me, I got "apoplectic," which means "liable to fits of rage in which the face becomes very red." Probably, Barry was frustrated that we weren't all friends.

Then, when I asked how Myrna was feeling about me, I got the word "stern." The definition is "firm, strict, or uncompromising." From this, I concluded that her pattern of thought was strict and uncompromising. This seemed to fit. Myrna definitely did not like me, and she wouldn't change her mind about it. Some of the other words I got on Myrna told me that Myrna would accept my offer to bring powerful introductions to her husband and daughter, if I pursued her. However, her acceptance wouldn't necessarily constitute a friendship. I didn't want to be hurt anymore, so I decided not to pursue her.

Sometimes I would question the morality of my actions. Since I had never heard of this ability to read other people's minds through words, I didn't know if it was right to continue. All along, Janet had been encouraging me to use this aspect of my gift for good purposes and not to do it for snooping into other people's thoughts. But, being human, I definitely enjoyed having the edge on the relationship between Chuck and me and Barry and Myrna. I could gain direct access to their thoughts by calling up words on them. I decided to ask Carol's opinion as to the morality of my word-pulling.

I asked Carol, "Should I be doing this? Is this sick

behavior?"

She had a quick answer. "Hey, if I could do it, I would." Her answer gave me more reason to appreciate the gift I now had, although I hoped I wasn't misusing it.

Carol asked how I was feeling about what happened with Barry and Myrna because she knew how psychically connected I was to Barry. I told Carol that I couldn't believe that Myrna allowed her own insecurities to outweigh my offers. It was a break that comes along once in a lifetime. Carol said it was too bad Myrna hadn't taken me up on my offers. She laughed as she said, "When their kids grow up, if they would ever get divorced, there would have been a lot more money to split up. Most of the women around here use plastic surgeons in New York City rather than Philadelphia."

I had to admit to Carol that I was kind of glad my offer wasn't accepted. One reason had to do with the fact that Myrna really didn't like me, and one trip to New York would not have changed her mind. Carol agreed. "That's right. You got the word 'stern' on her."

Gradually, I was realizing that this might be a unique talent--average housewife Linda Gilman develops a talent previously unheard of. I only had a junior college degree, but I could come up with words that were graduate level. I could fly and nobody else could. What more did I want?

# Chapter 12

I was now recovering and feeling normal again for the first time since my catharsis began. In actuality, I was starting to transform myself into the better person that I had always talked about. Change takes time. I began by gradually gaining back some of my weight. I also tried to gain back confidence in myself.

In July, I went to my niece's wedding, and I surprised everyone by leading a conga line around the entire ballroom. Since my mind was now healthier, I was able to teach myself how to gain back this confidence. I remembered a saying that I had made up once, one that I had always lived by. It may have been a take-off on the story of Rumplestiltskin, who spun straw into gold. Mine says, "Spin manure into gold." To me, this means that if something less than good happens, I should make it work for me and not against me. Therefore, I look at everything bad that happened to me during my catharsis as having occurred to make me a better person and to help me overcome my fears.

I tried to reconsider the Kramer situation. Sometimes, I would imagine I was either Barry or Myrna, and I would look at myself through their eyes. For the first time, I could see how they may have seen me as a threat. Perhaps they misunderstood my motives for wanting to help them. Maybe they thought I was trying to control their lives and that I was too domineering. While I may never know what they really thought of me, I found it amusing that someone actually may have felt threatened by me.

I was learning to see myself differently. Whenever I reviewed my lifetime accomplishments, I was very proud. I think that it was at this time that I really began to cherish life. I had so much to live for. After nearly dying during my catharsis, I had now begun to regard life as a challenge rather than as a sickness. I knew that I never would want to die again.

As the trip to Chicago and L.A. was getting closer, I was starting to get nervous. Even though the Old Lady had told me that the rich and famous would like me, I still didn't know what it was that they would like about me. This was to be the first test to see whether or not I had actually become different. Another thing making me nervous was the thought of having to take several plane rides. I have always had a fear of planes. But I knew I would be able to reason away this fear. First, I reminded myself that I had already known of the only two disasters that had occurred in my life before they actually happened. If I had been warned about my father's death and my own catharsis, then it stood to reason that I would be forewarned about any danger related to the plane rides. It was quite obvious to me that whoever the spirits were that guided me, they were definitely out to help me. From pursuing this logic, I was able to drop my irrational fear of flying.

Before we left for Chicago, I planned my course of action. I decided that I would be outgoing instead of shy. I called my mother to thank her for helping me through my childhood shyness. When I realized that she had confidence in me, it was easier to have confidence in myself.

I also decided to risk telling people about my experiences. I knew some people would be turned off and find me weird. Others would like me. Some would be helped by my story. One thing I knew for sure--nobody would forget me with the story I had to tell.

Just as I predicted, not everyone who heard my story

was happy to hear it. But I had practice dealing with rejection from Myrna, who was a master of rejecting people. Some people were absolutely fascinated with my story, and those people made the risk worthwhile.

From Chicago, we flew to Los Angeles. We arrived in L.A. the day before the Greenberg's anniversary. After getting settled, we went to one of Robert's houses in the little red sports car we rented for the week. It occurred to me that I hadn't seen or spoken to Robert in about five years. When we arrived at their home, Robert and his wife Susan were very hospitable to us. They served us drinks as we relaxed in their casual yet comfortable beach house.

After we talked a little about our visit to Chicago, Robert began to tell us about a house he was in the process of building. It was to be four stories high with a swimming pool on the roof. The elevator was still under construction. After seeing our interest in such an unusual house, he asked us if we wanted to walk to the next block to see it. As much as I would have enjoyed seeing the house, I told Robert that this might be a good chance for me to get to know Susan better, and I had to admit that I had a fear of heights. Climbing up four stories of a house under construction would be a very unpleasant experience for me. "You'll have more fun without me," I said as I encouraged the two men to visit the house.

I really enjoyed getting to know Susan. We talked about the new business she had started. Although she didn't need the money, Susan enjoyed using her creativity, and she loved interacting with people. She had opened a beauty salon called, "Head West." She told me that the "W" was made out of two horseshoes welded together.

Chuck and Robert seemed to be gone for quite some time. When they returned, Chuck's face was as white as a ghost's. Knowing something was wrong, I asked, "Chuck, what's the matter?"

In a very calm voice, he answered, "Linda, while Robert was walking me through the house, he showed me two places where he is putting in 'teepee skylights.'" Suddenly, the second stage of my past-life experience had caught up with me.

After I had encountered Barry in the woods with his tribe, I went back to my own tribe. I walked into the shaman's teepee. Inside, the teepee was dark. Robert was dancing in front of the fire. All of the Indians were throwing their worldly goods at him.

I told him what I had done. I thought he would be angry with me. But, instead, he stopped dancing, looked at me, and put his hands on me in blessing.

Now, my face drained. It must have been whiter than Chuck's. I was amazed at how the teepee skylights in Robert's new home fit right in with my vision. As Chuck continued to describe the house, he mentioned that Robert had the skylights custom-made, which proved to me that their existence in his house was no accident. After all, it's not like you can go into a building supply store and choose from round, square, or teepee windows.

At this point, I could no longer contain my excitement. I looked directly at Robert. "I have something to tell you. I had a vision of a past life, and you were in it." I then explained the entire vision, all the time feeling that he might think I was nuts. Although he listened politely, at the end he said he wasn't interested.

However, a few minutes later, out of the clear blue he told me that his favorite number was the Number Four. Susan said it was her favorite number, also. I couldn't reply. How could I possibly begin to make them understand how that number played such a significant role in my life? Instead, I said, "The Number Four stands for power."

The next day, Chuck and I were seated with Robert on the front deck of Robert's beach house overlooking the strand. There was a constant stream of beautiful young girls in thong bikinis roller-blading past us. I made a wise remark to the men about how I would have to get Chuck out of here. Robert turned to me and said, "Just because a man has a work of art doesn't mean that he can't look at other paintings." This compliment, coupled with the fact that Robert had taken to calling me, "Queenie," signified his approval of me. I really wanted him to like me because of how much he had done for our business and because he, like Barry, was an integral part of my vision during my catharsis. Was his approval of me actually the thing of importance that he had bestowed on me in the teepee? Maybe the blessing he gave me was really his mark of approval.

One day during our trip, while Robert was away on business, Susan invited us to her sprawling ranch in Hidden Hills. She told us it was originally the Marvin Gaye mansion. We needed a car to tour the grounds from the tennis courts to the stables. It was one of the most magnificent houses I had ever seen. She made me laugh when she told me that her big screen TV which comes up out of the bedroom floor once got stuck in the floor while it was turned on. In the middle of their bedroom stood a life-size stuffed horse. It was three colors, just like the painted pony in my vision.

The next day, I went with Chuck to a business meeting with a very handsome fashion designer named Rick Pallack. Rick owns a famous retail store where most of the male stars in Hollywood buy their personal wardrobes. Rick also dresses other famous people who aren't associated with Hollywood. All over his office are pictures of himself next to these stars. I immediately thought of the Old Lady telling me about the rich and famous. Maybe this knowledge is what gave me more confidence. Whatever it was, Rick, Chuck, and I seemed to enjoy each other's company.

One of the most exciting events of the trip was Robert and Susan's twenty-fifth wedding anniversary party on a gigantic yacht out of Marina Del Ray. Its three decks were filled with exciting people, wonderful food and drink, and great music. I even came out of my shell and was dancing the night away with Chuck on the top deck as the yacht cruised through the water. But most profound to me was the sight of Robert dancing around as everyone gave him fabulous gifts. It was like a modern-day version of my vision.

By the end of our vacation in California, I was already feeling like a different person. I had gained more confidence in myself, and I was better able to accept what had happened to me. For the first time, I was really beginning to believe that my past-life vision was real and that I was not crazy. Also, I was beginning to realize that most people will like me if I am just myself.

I couldn't wait to get back. I told everybody who would listen about Robert's teepee skylights and about the party on his yacht. It might have been my renewed enthusiasm, but people started to pay more attention to me, as if what I had proclaimed earlier might not be so crazy. Now that Part One of my vision, where Barry and I were from warring tribes, and Part Two, the shaman in the teepee, had both played out, my psychic powers were more of a recognizable force to those who had earlier doubted me. I was proud when Mary Ann, who had diagnosed me as having psychotic episodes, now changed her diagnosis to psychic. Even Carol, who had always made jokes about my experiences, was starting to believe in them. She said there was too much evidence for her not to take them seriously. So, for the first time in my life, I was getting respect for being a psychic person.

Now that the pain from my Catharsis Stage was behind me, I entered into what I call the Exploration Stage of my psychic transformation. The trip to California had made me realize that the clues to unraveling my psychic powers were out there, but it was up to me to find them. As a healthy person, I must now analyze what had happened to me. I must figure out what purposes such a power could serve.

Although I was getting stronger both physically and mentally, I was still crying nearly every day. But I found that I was developing the ability to remove myself from the pain that surrounded each event. In other words, I could look at my experiences from an objective viewpoint and not let my emotions get in the way. In doing so, I discovered there was a real significance to the order in which these experiences occurred.

Each major psychic occurrence followed shortly after each wave of suicidal feelings. I remembered that after my first wave, I experienced my past-life memory in three stages. After my second suicidal wave, I acquired the ability to pull up words on people. Finally, after my third wave, I had my near-death, out-of-body experience. The sequence in which these experiences occurred made me realize that I had to hit rock-bottom, in terms of layers of pain, until I could be brought up to the surface for a breath of psychic air.

Although I had begun by pulling words on Barry and Myrna, I had now moved beyond them. One day, I asked what Mary Ann was thinking, and I got the word "distraught," which means "in a state of distraction." I decided to call her that same day, Wednesday, but she was not home. Three days had passed before I could reach her. We talked for a while, then I asked her if she had been distraught on Wednesday.

She told me, "Linda, that is a perfect word to describe how I was feeling because I was in terrible pain that entire day." She had been several months pregnant at the time, and she told me she gone in for amniocenteses and that the doctors had not used anesthesia on her as she had expected them to. She told me my word-pulling was "scary." I laughed, telling her not to worry.

"So far, it hasn't hurt me," I reassured her.

Encouraged by my experiment on Mary Ann, I pulled up a word on Carol while she was on a business trip with her husband. As far as I knew, they were in Florida enjoying the nice weather. I asked how Carol was feeling and got the word "metamorphosis," which means "complete transformation of character, purpose, circumstances, etc." I couldn't wait for Carol to return home so I could check out "metamorphosis." When she came over, I asked her about her vacation. She said, "For one thing, we never stayed in Florida. We went to Nassau instead, and we didn't like our first hotel. Then, when we got to our second, we found that it was just as bad. We didn't even like our third hotel."

Then, I told Carol about "metamorphosis." She was amazed. As we talked, I told her that my psychic ability was more of a general ability. I seemed to summarize people's thoughts rather than knowing exactly what a person was thinking at a specific time and place.

This made me feel better regarding any moral implications. I wasn't directly eavesdropping. I was just sort of checking in for a "weather report."

One last example of my budding ability involved my son, Jarod. Jarod and his friends, Scott and Guy, had taken a third friend, Jeff, out to celebrate Jeff's twenty-first birthday. Usually, Jarod calls me if he is going to be out later than 3 a.m. I was still up at 3 a.m., and he hadn't called. Now it was 3:30, and still no call. As I started to worry, I decided to get some psychic help.

I pulled up a word on Jarod. I got "responsible," which eased my mind.

When Jarod finally returned home at 4 a.m., he told me that he and his friends had been bar-hopping all night, and that by the end of the night, nobody could remember where they had parked Jeff's car.

By this time, Jeff was very drunk and on the verge of passing out, so Jarod stayed with him while Scott and Guy went to look for the car. After about an hour and a half, Scott and Guy came back without the car. Jarod told Guy to stay with Jeff, and he and Scott went to look for the car. Within ten minutes, Jarod located it. Then, since Jarod was the only one who hadn't had anything to drink, he drove everybody home in Jeff's car.

When I told Jarod about the word "responsible," he said I couldn't have picked a better word. I replied, "I didn't pick the word--it was given to me."

So much was being revealed to me, but I still had one unanswered question: What about the third part of the vision? In the third part, I had walked out onto the field, and I was the special one. Barry and I had become friends. But, in this life, it didn't look like we would be having much of a friendship. The end of summer was approaching, and I had not heard from Barry and Myrna. I had no way of finding out whether or not Myrna had ever told Barry about our offer.

Even though they knew I had been sick, they never expressed any concern for my well-being. I thought that Barry, as a doctor, would want to know how I was doing. Maybe Barry had never believed that I was sick. Even if Barry had wanted to be friends, Myrna clearly did not, and there was nothing I could do about it. Could Barry and Myrna ever become our friends in this life?

For the answer to this one, I decided to consult the Old Lady. I walked into her hut where she was sitting quietly. "Will I ever see Barry again?"

She replied, "When you can stand on your own two feet."

Then I asked, "Should I tell Barry what happened?"

Her answer to this was, "Not if you don't want to--only if you need to."

I realized that, at some level, I needed to tell Barry about what had happened to me. I just didn't know how or when I could tell him. Instead of becoming frustrated as I would have earlier in my life, I slowly learned to accept the idea of fate. I started to realize that everything I went through, from my father's death to Robert's teepee skylights, happened for one particular reason--to make me realize I am psychic. Also, I started to believe that all of life is fated to a certain degree.

For example, I believe that my father was supposed to die on August 30, 1988. How else could I have been forewarned of its occurrence? At the time, however, I didn't know it was a warning. Should I have another psychic dream, I will listen!

I believed that if I were to ever see Barry again, it would be because of fate. I knew in my heart that there was nothing I could do to change the situation or I would have done it already. Therefore, whether or not we would ever see each other again was something out of my control. I tended to think that Part Three of my past-life memory would come true and that we could possibly become friends some day. I believed this because Parts One and Two had already played out. I would have to leave the whole issue up to fate and not try to force something to happen. After all, things higher than people were communicating to me, and I would have to learn to trust them.

It was now late in August, and the four-year anniversary of my father's death was approaching. Not having visited my father's grave once since his death and realizing the significance of the Number Four in my life, I decided it was time to pay him a visit.

While he was living, he would always tell me, "Someday you'll be sorry when I die." In reality, it was he who was the sorry one. I knew this was true when he appeared in my basement. At that moment, I knew he hadn't been able to pass on to the next level until I could forgive him. Later on, I figured that my father used Barry Kramer to deliver the message that had enabled me to forgive him.

On the anniversary of my father's death, the whole family went to the graveyard. Jarod could not go with us because he had already left for college. We picked up my mother. As we were nearing the cemetery, it started to get very gloomy and windy outside. We heard on the radio that a storm was approaching.

When we arrived at the cemetery, we saw some threatening teenagers hanging around the area near my father's grave. We knew they were up to no good. For protection, Chuck took a metal pipe out of the car. The four of us walked over to my father's grave site. Because of the rough weather conditions, we stayed only long enough to pay our respects.

The strange thing about the whole episode was how it symbolized the relationship between my father and me. As the wind kicked up, I drew my coat tighter around me. It reminded me of the way I would go deeper inside myself as my father worked himself into a rage and erupted into an emotional storm, which would leave the family devastated. And, even though the teenagers hadn't done anything, their threatening manner made me restless, just the way my father's constant badgering of my brother turned my stomach as I imagined the violence that was to follow.

Gradually, I was making myself a better person. I became more outgoing, and I took an interest in other people's lives and problems. I began to swim in a bigger pond.

In October, I looked forward to Parents' Weekend at Jarod's college in Washington. Chuck had made friends with a General who was running the fund-raising for Nancy Reagan's "Just Say No" program. While in Washington, we planned to have dinner with the General and his wife.

During a previous visit, I really got to know the General's wife. She has the most unbelievable personality. She is extremely outgoing, rather attractive, and strikingly confident. Together, the two of them made me feel very relaxed and quite comfortable in their presence. In fact, I felt more comfortable with them than I feel with many people I have known for a much longer time.

Before Chuck and I went to their apartment, The General and his wife spent the afternoon playing tennis at

Sergeant Shriver's house.  Unaware of their plans to join us, Sergeant Shriver asked them if they wanted to stay for dinner since Eunice was on a plane and wouldn't be home until later.  At that point, the General's wife told him that they had plans to go out to dinner with us.

When the General's wife told us the story, I felt very complimented.  Here she had been looking forward to seeing me, and I had been so upset because narrow-minded Myrna Kramer didn't like me.  Even the General and his wife had no problem with psychic phenomena, which only proved that I should be myself.  Some wouldn't like me, but others would.

Not long after our trip to Washington, I discovered that I needed surgery again.  I had many saliva glands in my mouth that were not functioning properly, so I had to remove nine of the worst ones.

When I went in for the surgery, I didn't know what to expect.  Would this new surgeon be someone from my past life?  Would I again wake up in my stomach?  Would I have flashbacks to my childhood surgery?

As it turned out, it was only a minor surgery.  I was sick for only a few days afterwards--no past life recollections...no psychic occurrences...no flashbacks.  It was a normal surgery that happened and was done with in short order.

This surgery made me realize that my connection to Barry was a karmic tie from another lifetime.  It had nothing to do with the fact that I needed surgery.  Now, I know that I can have future surgeries without the worry that what happened with Barry will happen again.

Ironically, I noted an interesting contradicton between my scar revision and my saliva gland surgeries.  The visible yet painless scar from my childhood surgery concealed the traumas of my past. When I attempted to make the scar less visible, these traumas were unleashed. However, the saliva gland surgery possessed a feeling all its own. The doctor sliced through some nerve endings in my lip, leaving me with a permanent tingling sensation. This sensation is a constant reminder of the scar, but that doesn't bother me. Although I can feel this scar with my tongue, this time the scar is hidden.

## Chapter 13

That year, 1992, we took a family vacation to Puerto Rico over the Christmas holidays. I met many interesting people, and I told almost everyone I met about my story. Most people either weren't very interested, or they really enjoyed the topic and shared some of their own experiences.

Only one person offered her opinion as to what happened that was very different from any I had heard before. This woman was a writer and seemed very intelligent. She told me that my past-life vision wasn't a memory from a past life at all. She said it was actually a pre-cognitive vision, or a vision of the future. Because I am, by no means, an expert on psychic phenomena, I really didn't know how to evaluate her statement. However, what I did know was that whatever it had been, my vision was certainly the strangest thing I had ever heard of.

Apparently, my vision was unusual enough to interest others. I was encouraged by people's reactions. I felt that somehow I had been given this gift to share with others, and telling the story was one way to share it.

With this mission in mind, I went to Janet's annual New Year's Eve party. There I encountered a couple, a psychiatrist and his wife, whom I had known only casually. I decided to tell the psychiatrist about my experiences to see if he would think I was crazy. I began telling him about the words and then about my past-life recall. He seemed very attentive, so I continued about my psychic dream and everything else related to what I now considered to be my gift.

Instead of telling me I should be locked away, he said something quite to the contrary. He told me that he had both heard about this and read about it. But he warned me that it was very rare. "For some reason, at certain times, people need something like this to happen to them in their lives." When I asked him if it would stay with me, he said he felt it could go away.

Thinking I might lose this precious gift, I was suddenly feeling very protective over it. After we talked some more, I told him I realized he was right. I did need these experiences to happen to me so that I could become the person I have always wanted to be.

What surprised me, though, was that a psychiatrist, who is a medical doctor by degree, could actually believe in the possibility of psychic occurrences. He also gave me another valuable piece of advice: he urged me to get in touch with either Temple University or the University of Pennsylvania to find out about the courses they offer on psychic phenomena. I thanked him for the information, but I decided I wasn't quite ready to take the courses. However, I was ready to do more investigating on my own.

Not long afterwards, I made an appointment with a well-known local astrologer, Shirley Kiley, to have my astrology chart done. Shirley told me that I have a very fortunate chart. She said I am an old soul. When I asked her what that meant, she told me that I have lived many lives before this present one, and I have arrived at a high spiritual level in this incarnation in which I was chosen to receive this gift.

She said that Chuck and I were lovers in another lifetime, but we never got married because I could exercise more power as his concubine than I could as his wife. I told her that we had an incredible marriage. She said she could tell this because my chart showed that we were able to work out a lot of our problems from a past lifetime. One of the problems was that we had lost a child. Because of this loss, our children would be very precious to us in this lifetime.

Shirley had done so well telling me about my personal life that I decided to ask about how Robert Greenberg fit into my life. She explained to me that I came into this life without owing a lot of karma. Instead, I had a lot of karma owed to me. Despite the fact that a business relationship and a friendship had materialized between Chuck and Robert, the connection between Robert and me happened because it was owed to me from a previous life.

Not only was I impressed with Shirley, but Chuck was giving her his whole attention. While looking at Shirley, he was pointing to me and saying, "She thinks just because she has seen a few major bad events before they happened that every time something really bad is going to happen, she'll know about it. For example, if she is supposed to get on a plane that is going to crash, she'll know about it ahead of time. Isn't that the most ridiculous thing you've ever heard?"

Shirley looked at Chuck and, in a very confident tone of voice, she said, "She will know."

Shirley seemed to understand me better than I understood myself. She went on to talk about the energy center of my soul, which she called my chackra. She told me that my last chackra had opened up and with it had come the opening of my third eye, or psychic power.

Even though I am psychic, my powers are in the infancy stage. However, she assured me that they will grow and grow and that I will become more psychic as time goes by. She predicted that, by 1995, I will be having feelings about other people and even about world figures. Also, from now on, I would feel like I am going through life in a first-class seat. Since I will know of things in advance, I will no longer have to suffer the same things other people will have to suffer. Finally, she told me that this was my last life and, because it is my last, I will not have a violent death. Instead, I will pass gently over to the other side, and I can basically choose when I wish to die. When she revealed this, I remembered that the Old Lady had told me something similar a while back.

I must say that I felt kind of funny after leaving Shirley's office. Everything she had said sounded really good, but it was a lot to take in at one time. But I took comfort in the fact that she had understood me. Apparently, I wasn't so strange to everybody, only to those who didn't understand. Maybe this odd duck wasn't so odd.

The visit to Shirley Kiley did not quench my thirst for knowledge. It only whetted my appetite. I decided to take up my reading again, and I remembered Ellen's recommendation that I read a book called Many Lives, Many Masters by Brian L. Weiss. Weiss, who is a psychiatrist, talks about a patient whom he hypnotized in a effort to rid the patient of her fears. While she is under hypnosis, the patient begins to regress to former lifetimes. Also, a spirit starts to speak through her, telling Weiss things about his own life which she could not possibly have been privy to. For example, Weiss had a baby who developed a heart problem. Through her, the spirit told him what the problem was and why it had happened. Completely amazed by his experience with this woman, Weiss continued to work with past-life regressions on many other people.

Many Lives, Many Masters confirmed something for me. Through reading this book and comparing my experience with that of his patients, I now knew that I was not crazy in calling my experience a past-life recollection. In fact, I was now quite sure that all of my experiences had been both real and purposeful. Certainly, the result of everything that has happened to me has been positive from the way I had handled Barry and Myrna to the way I have been opening up to strangers. As a result, I began to understand that this gift, which I had hated so much during my catharsis, was really here for my betterment. Something higher than people was communicating to me, and this something told me, "This is a gift to be enjoyed, not to be feared."

It was now January of 1993, and it had been almost a year since my nervous breakdown had begun. By this time, I was completely over all of the pain that had resulted or, at least, as over it as I was ever going to get. I was back to a healthy ninety-five pounds, a weight I was able to maintain for the last six months. One of the reasons I was able to remain stable at this weight was that I was exercising for two hours every day. Even though I still went through short periods of crying and mild depressions, I was the healthiest that I had been, both physically and mentally, in a long time.

The most difficult part for me now was having to accept that these experiences were real and that I was a different person because of them. I would never be able to return to the way I was before because now I knew things that other people didn't. Some people told me that the experiences I had described to them were called, "peak experiences." Maybe they were my peak experiences, or maybe there were higher ones yet to come. Either way, I had gone beyond anything I, or anyone else I knew, had ever heard of. I began to feel that getting over the peak was an accomplishment in itself.

On January 23, Chuck and I went out to dinner with Janet and a business associate of hers named Dave. At the time, Janet was working on her album which she produced with Dave, who owned a recording studio. They said they needed our input on business issues relating to the album and its distribution, so she invited us to dinner. Chuck and I were happy to meet them, and we suggested a nice Italian restaurant.

When we got to the restaurant, we were surprised when the maitre'd told us there was a forty-five minute wait. Dave said he had to be home early, and he wouldn't be able to wait that long. Janet knew a Greek restaurant in the same shopping center, so we walked over there.

We were glad that it was a lot less crowded. There were a few tables to the left, and then there was a dividing wall which prevented you from seeing most of the front section. The restaurant was quite empty, which I said was unusual for most restaurants in our area on a Saturday night. Only a few families were there.

I was following Janet and Dave to the back section where we were to be seated. For some reason, I looked behind me and noticed that Chuck wasn't there. The reason I couldn't see him was that he was on the other side of the half-wall that divided the two sides of the restaurant. Even though I couldn't see him, I recognized his voice saying, "Hi, how are you doing?" By his tone, I knew he had met someone we knew very well. I wondered who he would be talking to in this out-of-the-way restaurant.

I walked across the empty restaurant and turned when I reached the half-wall. As I walked around it, I stopped dead in my tracks. There was Barry and Myrna. They were with their son and another couple with a baby.

All of a sudden, my heart started to pound

uncontrollably. My mind flashed back to when I had asked the Old Lady if I would ever see them again, and she had said, "Yes, when you can stand on your own two feet." Well, here I was feeling much better, and there they were!

Not knowing what to do, I just stood there. Chuck grabbed my hand and pulled me over. As I was getting closer to them, my story began to flood my head. Now I was standing right at their table. Myrna was seated the closest to where I was standing. She looked up at me, "Hi, how are you feeling?"

Her question gave me the answer as to whether or not they had realized I was sick. It was easy to figure out that if they had known I was sick, and they hadn't bothered to get in touch, then they really didn't care about me. I answered, "fine," without any emotion, as if the question were meaningless and just a cliche.

"So, how are the boys?" was her next question. I began to talk about them as if I were filling in time while my brain followed another track. It was now or never. I might not see them for another couple of years, so I had to do something in the next two minutes or forever regret it.

Instantly, I formed a plan. In the middle of our conversation, I abruptly broke eye contact with Myrna, took off my jacket, swung it over my right shoulder, and swayed my left hip out to the side. I picked up my head and looked straight into Barry's eyes.

"I have a story I want to tell you some day."

He said, "Okay."

Immediately, Myrna changed the subject and began to talk about the baby at the table. While Myrna talked, I picked up my head again, looked at her and said, without feeling it, "It was nice seeing you."

Then, I spun around, and Chuck and I both left. I was

confident that I had delivered my message. If they didn't want me, then they couldn't have me. I went back to my table and sat down with my real friends.

After I had a couple of days to think about the incident, I began to realize that this incident was, in effect, a part of the third stage of my past-life vision. In the vision, I walked outside of the tent after Robert blessed me. The sun shone. I walked across an empty field. Some of my tribe were following beside me. At the end of the field was the beginning of the trees. There stood Barry. He was on foot, holding the rope on his horse. The red-brown feather in his headpiece was pointed down. His hair was long and parted in the middle. Some of his tribe was with him. He seemed to be the son of the chief. They all stared at me, and I was the special one. And, then, Barry and I were friends.

All that had just happened was enough to make a connection to the vision. I had walked across an empty restaurant. Some of my tribe were with me. Barry was sitting with his back to the wall with some of his tribe. They all stared at me since I was the focus of attention. He was seated at the place of honor at the table. When I told him that I had a story to tell him, he said, "Okay," which meant he was receptive to seeing me again.

A few days later, I decided to do some words on them so that their relationship with me might seem clearer. On Myrna, I got "cathartic." "Cathartic" is "a purging of pent-up, socially unacceptable emotions or truths." Maybe Myrna was releasing a pent-up truth to Barry. I believed that if she hadn't already told him about the offer I had made to her, then possibly she was going to tell him now. On Barry, I got the word "remorseful," which means "full of deep and painful regret for one's wrongdoing." This told me that he felt bad that, since it hadn't worked out between us socially, I had never gotten the chance to tell him the story I wanted to tell him.

On January 28th, I got a very interesting word on Myrna. The word was "correspondence." My birthday was only two days away, and I knew they had a record of my birthday in their office. If my word was correct, then I figured that they were probably sending me a birthday card. But after all that had happened, a birthday card was the last thing I would expect from them.

When I got the envelope in the mail from Myrna the next day, I just couldn't believe it. The envelope was post-marked on the 28th, and inside the envelope was a birthday card. The first thing I noticed was that it was the type of card that is bought in a package of many cards for the purpose of not having to go out to buy a card every time someone has a birthday. I buy these packages of cards, too. The card read, "Wishing you a happy birthday on this special day and always." It was signed, "Love, Barry and Myrna." To me, the "and always" part meant "Have a good life; we don't wish you any harm, but we also don't want you in our lives." The words were getting exciting, so I kept on going.

On February 1st, I got "recognition" on Barry. I found out that one of the definitions of "recognition" fit the situation perfectly. It was "formal acknowledgment of a person's right to speak at a particular time." From this, I deduced that Barry would let me tell him my story, if the circumstances should arise.

The next day, I got "reflective" on Barry and "respect" on Myrna. Coincidentally, all the words started with "r." On the 9th of February, I got a word on Myrna that was actually two words coming out as one word. The word was "correspondence-invitational." I took out a piece of paper and wrote down, "Myrna, February 9, correspondence-invitational." On the 12th of the month, my words came true.

That day Jarod brought in the mail. He handed me a letter with Myrna's handwriting on the envelope. Before I even gave myself a chance to blink, I uncontrollably yelled, "Boys, stop what you're doing. Please, stop what you're doing. Come here and be my witnesses. Come upstairs with me while I prove I was right." The boys stopped what they were doing and came upstairs. First, I showed them the piece of paper that said, "Myrna, February 9, correspondence-invitational." Then, as I was looking at the letter, I noticed it was postmarked on February 11th, Chuck's birthday.

The fact that it was not postmarked February 9th proved only a temporary setback. I tore open the envelope in front of my boys. Inside was a birthday card with a picture of Father Time sticking up his middle finger--a humorous picture, joking that it's too bad you're getting older. I opened the card and saw the words, "Dear Chuck, I hope we can get together soon. Love, Barry and Myrna."

Even though this card was not postmarked on February 9th, the day I got the words "correspondence-invitational," it was quite obvious that this was a store-bought card. It was possible that she could have gone out to hand pick this card on that day and then mailed it two days later. She wanted to say, "screw you" indirectly. I laughed because, unbeknownst to her, I already knew.

I couldn't wait for Chuck to get back from his business trip to show him my note and the card. His reaction was, "Wow!"

Once again, I went to visit the Old Lady. I walked into her shack and I was surprised that she wasn't sitting on the bare wooden bench as usual. This time, she was lying on a big feather comforter with her head on a pillow. I said, "You look so comfortable now."

She said, "I am comfortable now." At that point, she sat up and pulled aside the comforter to make room for me, saying, "Come here and sit next to me." She took one of her very thin arms and put it around my shoulder. I saw her bony fingers resting on the top of my arm.

Then, I turned back to her. "What did you do to me?"

She looked at me. "I had to take you back in order for you to go forward."

Immediately, I fell out of the trance. What she had said made perfect sense. This Old Lady, who for all intents and purposes was an extension of my soul, had to bring me back to my horrible childhood and back to another lifetime so that I could get rid of all the pain that was in me for all these years. Only then, after I had been brought back, could I move forward and start to reach my potential. Bringing me back to another lifetime and showing me how brave I was as an Indian warrior was her way of helping me to be brave during my catharsis.

The Old Lady was confirming what Shirley Kiley had said, "It's not so important that you have this gift--what's important is what you're going to do with it." I could no longer ignore making a decision as to what direction I would move with this gift.

One option I had was to use my ability to pull up words to help other people. But I had neither the time nor the desire to do so. I felt as if I would be trapped into performing. When I discussed this with Carol, she told me, "Linda, you're not a performing bear." What could I do? Open up a word stand?

Maybe what I should be doing is finishing my mission

with Barry. How would I tell him the story so it would all make sense? At a restaurant? No. There would be too many interruptions. Besides, Myrna made it pretty clear that she wouldn't want to be there with me.

I needed uninterrupted time to tell the whole story and to let it unfold as it happened. Then I hit upon an unlikely situation. I could go to his office, shuffle his patients, and have him schedule me for a two-hour session in which I would tell him everything that had happened to me. Lots of luck! I decided not to answer the card.

The next step of my mission was to get in touch with the University of Pennsylvania. I had Chuck call up the university and tell them that his wife was having psychic experiences and wanted to know if there was someone at the university she could talk to.

The university said that no one in its faculty specialized in psychic phenomena. But Chuck was referred to a professor in Georgia, a Doctor William G. Roll, who had done his undergraduate work at Oxford University and later received his Ph.D. in psychology from a famous university in Sweden. The doctor had written his thesis on parapsychology. He had gone on to do work for television shows such as "Unsolved Mysteries" and "Sightings." His list of credentials was most impressive, and I looked forward to calling him.

I was able to speak to him for about forty-five minutes during which time I told him a good deal of my story. Right from the start, he was very supportive. He made me feel that this was something real and something very positive. He said that what had happened to me is a natural phenomenon and very common. He also said that most of the people who experience these phenomena have one thing in common--they have had a bad childhood and they turn inside of themselves. Then, I asked my usual question, "Professor, do you think I'm strange or weird?"

"No," he said. "You have a gift that is not strange or weird, but it is actually superior." Then I told him that at times I thought I was insane. "On the contrary, Linda, you're more than sane."

At that point, he asked about our family life. After telling him only a little bit, he interrupted to say that we sounded like a family of geniuses. I then told him excitedly that Chuck had been declared a genius in math by the University of Pennsylvania when he was only three years old, and that Jarod had gotten a 770 on his math S.A.T.'s and had received an academic scholarship to G.W.U. Michael, too, was on the same track academically and has an apparent business genius that was detectable since early childhood. I told him I knew I wasn't a genius.

"Ah, but you are! Your genius is your ability to comprehend everything that happens to you." I was taken aback. I certainly didn't feel like a genius. With minimum effort, I had gotten mediocre grades through high school, and I socialized my way through junior college. I only scored average on my S.A.T.'s. I'm a person with such a poor sense of direction that I can't even find my way out of our neighborhood sometimes. However, if Dr. Roll thinks I am a genius, then who am I to argue?

Before I got off the phone, I asked him what he thought I should do with my story. He threw the ball in my court, saying that since I was highly intuitive, I would figure out what to do.

As the end of winter approached, Chuck and I were busy planning for a combined trip to Las Vegas and Los Angeles in April. Chuck made an effort to locate two well-respected experts in parapsychology who lived in Los

Angeles by the names of Josh and Caren Stone.

I gave them a call. Caren answered. I told her some of what had happened to me. I could tell by her voice that she seemed interested in my story, so I told her I would be out in Los Angeles in April and asked whether I could make an appointment to see her and her husband. She invited me to visit them at their home.

After listening to my story, she labeled me as "clairvoyant," "clairaudient," and "psychic." The "clair" part of the words referred to "clarity." According to Caren, "voyant" refers to "sight," and "audient" refers to "auditory senses."

Of course, I was already learning what "psychic" meant. She said that schizophrenics and psychics share a common symptom. They both hear voices in their heads. For this reason, she told me I was fortunate that I had never gone to a mental hospital because, if I hadn't been able to prove I was psychic, they may have locked me up. She said that mental hospitals are filled with people who are psychic, but they are classified as "sick" because they are never able to prove they are psychic.

That same night, Chuck called from New York to check up on me. Before he had a chance to speak, I excitedly told him about my being clairvoyant, clairaudient, and psychic. Being a hundred miles away, his first question was, "Are you clairsexual, too?"

I laughed. "I don't know, but I promise to give it a try."

Then, Chuck told me about his meeting with Carol Horn, a designer he worked with during the mid '70's.

"I'm doing a sweater deal with her, " he said. Chuck told me that had related some of my psychic experiences to Carol. "She was fascinated, Linda. She asked me to see her apartment because what she had there would interest us."

Chuck accepted the invitation and helped to carry up some coats the doorman had been holding for her when Chuck noticed that the coats were designed in Indian motif. When he commented about the design, she said some American Indians had made them for her as part of a recent business venture.

When Chuck stepped into the apartment, he was stunned! Twenty- eight stories above the streets of Manhattan, it was decorated like a Pueblo with one-foot thick adobe walls which had heavy timbers extending outward. Chuck had never seen anything like it. Surrounding him was a display of the most incredible collection of American Indian artifacts he had ever seen. There were authentic drums, feather and beaded headpieces used in ceremonies, fetish bowls, and hand-painted pottery.

He told me that the last thing to catch his attention was a wall picture of an Indian woman with large, soft, brown eyes, and long, dark, straight hair. "Linda, that woman in the picture looks just like you."

# Chapter 14

After so many months of intense self-discovery and healing, it was more than time for a little excitement! First, we would be off to Las Vegas. Chuck spent all day at the MAGIC Show, the menswear industry's semi-annual trade show. After a day of meetings, I would join Chuck for social dinners at night.

Then, it was off to Los Angeles where Chuck would conduct more business, and I would meet with the parapsychology experts. Socializing with the rich and famous was still a little unnerving to me, but, at the same time, I was ready.

When we arrived at the hotel in Las Vegas, one of the employees who recognized Chuck from his previous stays said, "Oh, you brought your wife this time."

As a gorgeous chorus girl walked by, Chuck replied, "Yeah, it's like bringing a sandwich to a banquet." I didn't like this remark very much; however, he was right about the banquet part. Going out to dinner with Chuck and his business associates every night was very much like being at a banquet of the very successful.

One of the people that we went out with was Rick Pallack. Of course, we remembered each other from our visit to California in the summer of 1992. Rick took us to Spago, a restaurant that is always crowded. It is nearly impossible to get a same- day reservation unless you're someone really important. Luckily, Rick knew the owner, Wolfgang Puck, so he not only got us a same-day reservation, he also got us a good table.

When we were seated, I started to tell Rick about some of my experiences because he previously told me that his girlfriend, Chantel, had given up a promising modeling and acting career to study parapsychology. Rick said that I had the most perfect experience because I was able to regurgitate all the big chunks of my life that had been bothering me.

I was so relaxed with Rick that I even started to open up about my insecurities. I confided to him that I was always nervous around high-profile people because I had come from a dysfunctional family, and I didn't like feel I belonged with them. At this point, Rick looked around the room. Then, he focused on one of the waiters. "Linda, look at that waiter. Now look at all these people sitting down who own big companies. Many of the people here are rich and famous. But that doesn't mean they're better than that waiter. The only difference is that these people being waited on have had more experiences which make them more interesting, but not necessarily better."

I thought this was a great way of looking at things, and it helped me to change my thinking.

When I started to talk about how Robert fit into my experiences, Rick interrupted me. "Isn't that Robert at the next table?" I leaned over to see, and sure enough, there was my shaman. He was seated at a big table surrounded by lots of people. I waved. Then, he came over to us. He gave me a big hug and a kiss before he went to talk to Chuck.

While they were talking, I commented to Rick, "You know, it's funny. I haven't seen Robert in nine months, and there's lots I would like to say to him. But I can't possibly tell him what I want to under these circumstances. There are too many people around."

Rick replied, "With some people, you don't have to talk to them. You can just look at them, and you know that there is all this underlying stuff which makes words unnecessary." I understood what he was saying: knowledge between two people can still be there, even if words aren't.

Speaking with Rick and hearing his philosophy gave me the confidence I needed to face the rest of the trip. I would be meeting powerful people in Chuck's industry. If I could make myself see them as just plain, regular people, I would be able to be myself, and they would like me for who I am.

My plan to be myself worked better than I expected. Chuck and I saw some of these people at night as we visited the casinos, and they flipped over me. Men that hadn't talked to Chuck in the past were now talking to him because of me. Also, I was opening up about my psychic experiences, and people were fascinated.

One man was so interested in my experiences that he wouldn't let go of my hand. He just kept holding on to it. I pulled away again and again, but he kept holding on even tighter until I finally said, "Would you like me to cut it off at the wrist so you can take it back to your room with you?" At that point, he got the message.

Later, I found out that this man never returned any of Chuck's calls. "I'm glad you got his attention, Linda. But don't think it was because of your  psychic experiences-- you could have been reading the dictionary backwards, and he would not have noticed."

"Guess I turned out to be the best sandwich you ever brought to a banquet!" I retorted, referring to Chuck's comment when we first checked in to the hotel.

Another night, we went out to dinner with Robert and Susan. During dinner, Robert said that he had something to tell me later. After dinner, we all went to the Mirage Casino. When I told Robert that this was my very first time in Las Vegas, he decided to take me over to the craps table and show me how to play. He didn't do a very good job since we lost all our money. Chuck laughed, "I can't believe a psychic and a shaman together couldn't win any money!"

Robert didn't care. We tried some more. At one point, he smiled and said, "Well, you're rolling the dice in Las Vegas, kid." I wanted to say, "Yeah, and look who I'm with--a man who built a billion-dollar business!" I felt on top of the world.

Later, Robert pulled me aside and told me about the recent death of his father, which had been quite sudden. "Linda, one month before my father died, I had very strong feelings about his impending death. Because of these feelings, I called him every day to check on him." Robert explained to me that this situation had made him more open- minded to my psychic claims.

"Robert, I think you have psychic ability proved by your great accomplishments. But, in your world, they call it business sense."

It was Robert's entrepreneurial genius that now had him building a successful company the second time. When L.A. Gear reached the nine hundred million dollar mark, there was a need to bring in outside financing. Trefoil Capital, an investment group funded primarily by Disney family money, put $100 million into L.A. Gear. They immediately replaced most of the regime with Trefoil's own people. Robert knew it was time to move on. In the meantime, Chuck had been one of the only people that Trefoil chose to keep on board. He was one of the few whose contract was renewed.

Robert would not let the situation get him down. Instead, Robert started a new company called "Skechers U.S.A." with his son, Michael. It is a shoe company that began by selling its own brands called "Skechers" and "Sooo L.A." Eventually, Robert's company helped bring Dr. Martens from the limited markets of the Melrose and Soho districts to the department stores of New York and Los Angeles.

Dr. Martens became the "in" fashion in the suburbs. Robert said he believed that Dr. Martens were anti-fashion, and anti-fashion was fashion. He had the vision to bring the look of Dr. Martens into the mainstream.

While building his new company, Robert slowly began to bring back many of the people who were with him at L.A. Gear. He started with the people he felt most comfortable with. It seemed like he was bringing back his former trusted warriors to build a new tribe. He invited Chuck to license for him, but Chuck had to turn him down at that time. Chuck's new contract with L.A. Gear lasted through December of 1993, and it prohibited him from representing any other shoe company. I hoped he would come back into our lives, but we were leaving that up to fate.

After Chuck finished his business in Las Vegas, it was off to Los Angeles. As soon as we stepped off the plane, I called up the parapsychology experts to confirm my appointment. They said they would have to cancel because they had several emergencies involving people who needed to talk about their sick pets.

"You're cancelling me for sick pets?"

Caren answered, "Yes."

I was stunned, but if that was what was supposed to happen, my fate obviously did not include these people. All I said was, "Okay." I ended the conversation on a pleasant note.

During our stay in Los Angeles, Chuck and I went out

with a different couple each night. One night, we went out with Rick, who was back in L.A. He took us out to the original Spago in Hollywood, which is known for its celebrity clientele. Throughout the dinner, Rick introduced us to a variety of famous people who came over to our table to greet him. Among them were Ed Begley, Jr., a famous L.A. newscaster, and billionaire

Marvin Davis and his entourage. Even the owner, Wolfgang Puck, sat down with us.

At this dinner, Rick brought his then-current girlfriend, Chantel, with him. She was as gorgeous as Rick described her, and she was also incredibly friendly. When we were introduced, she said that she never goes to business dinners with Rick, but when Rick told her some of my story, she decided that she had to meet me. "I cancelled a very important meeting with two parapsychology experts who study with me in order to be with you."

I asked who the experts were. She told me a couple named Josh and Caren. I laughed and explained how these same people had cancelled me the day before so they could help some sick pets. "I think it's fate that you cancelled them to be with me."

Throughout the course of the dinner, I managed to tell my whole story to Chantel. She was very knowledgeable about what happened to me. First, she told me that when I was sick, all the crying, dancing, and meditating that I had done produced and overdose of endorphins which she claimed made me temporarily unbalanced.

Chantel had studied past-life memories and, according to her, my past-life memory was anything but crazy. She told me, "Barry was a warrior in another lifetime. He had his fun cutting up people. However, lifetimes are tit for tat; in this lifetime, Barry had to come back as a surgeon so that he could correct the mistakes he made." She also said that Myrna must have remembered me in her soul as the enemy while Barry remembered me as a friend.

"That is quite intriguing," I complimented her.

Concerning my ability to pull up words on people, Chantel said that the reason I was so heavily involved in this was because this new gift had become a great source of entertainment for me. When I thought about what she had said, I realized that she was absolutely right. When I started my word-pulling, I pulled up words on Barry and Myrna all the time because I had many issues with them, and it was fun. After I began to resolve those issues, though, I knew I would have to stop because I was afraid I might abuse this gift and then lose it forever. In a sense, I was developing a real attachment to it. I felt special as a result of this word-pulling ability.

The last topic Chantel felt very strongly about was my near death, out-of-body experience. She felt that the bearded figure I had seen on my T.V. wasn't necessarily Jesus, but it was probably a high, spiritual presence that wanted to show me the next realm.

She went on to say that had I expressed an interest in going to the next realm when the spirit had asked me, I would have had an out-of-body experience. "This is a high experience which I have had quite often. It is only offered to those who have made it to the Divine Order. You are now a part of the Divine Order."

She told me that people go to mountains and live in caves for years and years, waiting for such an experience. Here it was offered to me, and I had turned it down.

"What do you mean, the Divine Order?"

She answered, " Being in the Divine Order means that everything you need in life now starts to come your way."

If she was right and I was a part of this Divine Order, then there was still one thing I couldn't figure out--why me?

Before we left the restaurant, Chantel gave me one last bit of advice. She explained how the wires in my head and the wires in Barry and Myrna's heads were going crazy. She encouraged me to perform a ritual of releasing them. In my mind, I was to visualize this release. I had to let go of whatever issues I was holding on to, thereby stopping those wires. To make this process easier, she reminded me that "I never needed Barry," just like the second psychic dream had said.

I smiled. "You're right. Both in the dream and in reality, I didn't need Barry to get better. In the end, there was only one person who could save me--that was me."

Chantel clued me into some very important truths and some amazing possibilities that night. I left the dinner table with a tremendously positive feeling. In the days that I spent in Las Vegas and in Los Angeles, I believe that I changed from someone who was slightly ashamed of her gift to someone who was quite proud of it.

# Chapter 15

One day in March, I went with Chuck on a business trip to New York. We had decided to visit Carol Horn, so I finally would see her unique apartment. I felt very at home among her Indian artifacts. I told Chuck that I thought that the picture did look like me. After we got to know each other better, I told her that I was psychic. "Tell me about it," she urged.

"It's a long story," I warned her.

She invited us to make ourselves comfortable and told me to tell her whatever I wanted to. I could tell she was bright by the questions she was asking as I told her the story from beginning to end. She had good listening skills. She used active listening cues, such as saying, "Oh, my God!" or clutching herself when I would say something unbelievable.

When I finished, she told me that she thought that Barry and Myrna were only important to me because they happened to be the first people I read with my psychic abilities. If it hadn't been them, then it would have eventually been someone else. "You must do something with your story," she said. "You should go all the way with it."

I responded that my sister-in-law, Fleurette, had been telling me all along that I should write a book and that my friends had encouraged me to do so, as well, but I just couldn't picture myself doing it.

"I'm getting to the point where I have to do something because I am putting too much pressure on myself, pressure to somehow let Barry and Myrna know what happened and pressure to let other people know what happened without having to continually tell the story over and over again."

Carol encouraged me to turn my story into a book. "I'll talk to my friend. She is a writer and happens to be into psychic phenomena. I'll see if she would be interested in helping you write a book."

Right before we left, she asked if she could design the clothes if my story turns into a movie.

Something I have learned PC (Post Catharsis) is that human beings are resilient and can learn to accept just about anything. For example, I learned to accept not only my psychic ability, but also something that had bothered me my whole life--rejection. Now that I had something to talk about, it really didn't matter if one person didn't want to hear about it because there was a whole world out there who did.

In opening up to people, I have stretched myself by meeting new people and going to new places and, thereby, lost my fear of rejection. Furthermore, I have also discovered that there are many people out there who have had psychic experiences of their own.

I have found that if you open up to people, they will open up to you. For example, at a birthday party for my niece, I met a woman who had a psychic dream and didn't even know it. She dreamt that her sister had died in a plane crash. When she woke up that day, the woman decided that it was only a dream and completely blew it off, even though her sister was scheduled to fly home the next day on Pan Am flight 103.

For some reason, the friend with whom the sister was flying decided on a different destination at the last minute, and the two women cancelled their flights. Pan Am flight 103 blew up over Lockerbee, Scotland.

"Do you think it was a coincidence?" the woman had asked me after finishing her story.

"Absolutely not!" Then, I told her that when I had my first psychic dream, I had no idea what a psychic dream was. It wasn't until my second psychic dream that I realized the full implications of the first one. To me, this story reinforced the fact that psychic dreams are real, but people don't always recognize them for what they really are.

Another story came to me at random from the owner of a restaurant that Chuck and I frequent. The restaurant owner told us about a friend of his who had gone on a skiing expedition. While on the expedition, the friend had a very strong dream in which he was killed in an avalanche. He was so shaken that he told the others in his party about it and requested that he leave. The leader of the expedition denied his request, saying that they were in the middle of nowhere. On that very next day, the friend was killed in the avalanche.

Next, while I was visiting a local hair salon, a woman told me the story of her Jewish grandmother in Nazi Europe. Rather than sending her to a concentration camp, the grandmother and her family were sent to Siberia. Weakened, the family became very ill living in the frozen tundra. Then, one night, the grandmother had a dream that in one of the cabins, under a floorboard, sat a box containing enough money for the medicine the family needed to survive. Sure enough, the next day, the grandfather went to the cabin, checked under the floorboard, and found the box with the money they desperately needed.

Then, there have been a round of stories involving surgeries. One woman I happened to meet remembered what the doctor had said while she was under anesthesia. As soon as she woke, she told the doctor what she had heard. The doctor confirmed that everything she said was true.  But then he said, "You know, this is scientifically impossible."

Another woman said she had floated up to the ceiling and watched her entire surgery while she was under anesthesia.  When she told this story to others, though, they thought she was crazy.  No one would believe her, including the doctors.  However, she knew she wasn't crazy and that she had an out-of-body experience.

I also knew that the American Medical Association doesn't recognize such occurrences, but their opinions don't mean that these occurrences are not real.

My growing confidence basked in the warmth of summer.  I told my story to the wife of the prosecuting attorney in my town, and she grew very excited.  Another time, I went to New York with Chuck and shared my story as we walked through the Licensing Show.  As I finished telling my story to a man we had met there, an unfamiliar woman walked up to me and said, "Pardon me, but I overheard you telling your story, and I think it's the most fascinating thing I have ever heard.  I can't believe you live in the suburbs.  What a waste!  You should be living in the city where people can experience you and be around you."  Her words meant more to me than any I had heard in a long time.  I felt forty-six years of shyness melting away like an ice cube on a hot summer day.

Later in the afternoon, I happened to recall the concept that Jarod had taught me called, "Maslow's Hierarchy of Motivation."  When he first introduced me to this concept, I felt I had leveled off at the third stage, self-esteem.  Now I was fulfilling my self-esteem, and I was ready to move up a notch in the pyramid to the belongingness stage.  Eventually, after my belongingness needs are met, I can reach self-actualization, and I will be able to share a bench with the Old Lady.

Regardless of my stage, I knew that I had become a much happier person. I was still exercising for two hours and meditating for one hour each day. However, I wasn't crying anymore, not even periodically. For the first time in over a year, I could think about what had happened to me without shedding a single tear.

Along with this happiness came more feelings of kindness and compassion for other people. For a number of years, I protected myself by isolating my emotions. Now, I finally could express my own feelings, which enabled me to sympathize better with others. My inner voice often sang, "Love and understanding are what all humans crave." This was the phrase which had been communicated to me during my sickness. Now, I would use this phrase to keep me healthy forever.

Maybe everybody lives inside their heads, looking out through their eyes. So, where was reality? Inside or outside? This was a simple concept for me before, but now it took on much more depth. I used to always look at people and see their physical appearance. When I talk to people now, I am more aware of the fact that they are looking at me, probably wondering what I am thinking. Meanwhile, I am doing the same to them. Understanding this aspect of human behavior helped me to feel more secure in my personal interactions with people who otherwise may have made me insecure.

One night during the summer, Chuck and I went out to dinner with a Vietnamese couple with whom Chuck was doing business. I related my story to the business man's wife. She said that this was very common in her religion, but psychic dreams only come to those who are pure of heart. I had a hard time seeing myself as pure of heart since, in actuality, I am often selfish, self-centered, moody, and lazy. Still, I received the gift anyway. The question on my mind was, "Could one have these traits and still be pure of heart?"

Whether or not I was pure of heart, I always enjoyed doing good things for people by giving them the right advice. Even though I never knew I was psychic until 1988, I always had a great ability to see the consequences of actions. When faced with a problem, I instinctively know what to do to always come out on top. I don't know how I know these things, but I do, and I always share that knowledge with the people in my life.

In fact, everybody who has ever followed my advice has achieved good results. And, although my advice has provided wonderful things for people, I have never asked for money. In our business, Chuck and I make deals that create jobs for people, thereby changing their lives. In my religion, this is a very high thing to do. So, I believe that I am pure of heart to a certain degree, although I have always thought Chuck was more pure than me.

Probably the reason I got this gift is because I needed it, like the psychiatrist at the New Year's Eve party said. Jarod suggested that the spirits chose me because I have a clean slate. Having been a recluse most of my life, people don't know me very well. Therefore, when I come out and proclaim myself psychic, people will listen more because they don't know enough about me not to. Jarod also said that the spirits knew that if I could figure out how to get out of a bad childhood, I would also be able to figure out what to do with this gift.

I felt the responsibility to share this experience with the world because I knew my story could help people. I figured that it was too powerful to keep locked up in my mind. Not too long after our visit with Carol Horn, she called me to tell me that her writer friend, Eleanor, was interested in writing my book and would be calling me in the near future. Carol mentioned that Eleanor had won several awards in France for her writing.

Carol harmlessly suggested that I do a word on Eleanor just to see what I would come up with. I got the word "vituperative." Grabbing the dictionary, I told Carol the definition of vituperative. "Carol, my dictionary says it means 'verbally abusive.'" Carol quickly defended her friend by saying that Eleanor was the sweetest woman--an absolute doll--and that she was definitely not vituperative.

Within a couple of days, Eleanor called me. The first thing she said was that she heard that I had an incredible story. I said, "It's incredible because its true." I told her if she were to write it, all of the information would have to come from me. She acknowledged my remark and said that she would be willing to work with me.

"Come to New York next week," she said, "and we'll sign a contract."

That night, I couldn't sleep. I was completely mesmerized by the idea of revealing my life to the whole world. For forty-six years, I had been very private. Very few people knew about my life. Was I ready to go public? One other thing bothered me.

Everything about our conversation had been pleasant. There were no signs of her being "vituperative." All she had said was that I would tell her my story, and then we would sign a contract.

When I awoke the next day, Chuck said, "Linda, I've got bad news for you. Eleanor called this morning and said she couldn't do the book because it was non-fiction, and she could only do fiction."

Hearing this, I felt let down and angry. I wanted to tell her off. I sensed from what she had said to Chuck that the reason she didn't want to write my book is that she didn't want to play the role of a ghostwriter. What she really wanted to do was turn my life into a fiction story so she could get all of the credit. Well, she had her chance and she refused it. As far as the word "vituperative" was concerned, it really turned out to describe my thoughts towards her.

In retrospect, I finally decided that Eleanor was just not fated to write my book. I would have to find a new writer who could appreciate my story and who could deal with not receiving all the credit in order to be a part of something bigger than the writer.

The answer was right under my nose. It had to be my son, Jarod. Jarod had always been a writer. When he was little, he used to sit down with his brother and write funny stories that would have them both laughing all day. In school, Jarod would always get A's on his writings, and I used to save all of them so I could show them to my friends. He took creative writing in college, and, although he would complain that he didn't like writing, his professor told him he was a gifted writer and that he should do something with his ability in the future. I would now give Jarod the chance to do something with my story. We would form a partnership, and both our abilities would be tested.

Of course, I realized that summer was a time when Jarod would rather be playing sports and spending time with his friends. But, fate is fate. Still, I didn't want to scare him away, so I thought about how I could make his task easier. I asked Chuck if he would sit down with me, so I could record my words as I told him the story. Over the entire weekend, I recited as many details as possible.

Chuck helped me keep things in order.

When I thought I had told as much as I could possibly recall, Chuck offered to take the tape over to his typist, Judy, who eventually typed out sixty-three pages from my cassettes. When Judy finished her typing, she called Chuck's business line and asked for my number so she could speak to me. Judy began telling me that the story she typed for me was the most amazing story she had ever done, and she felt that she was working on the beginning stages of a masterpiece. She confided in me that her husband had died of a heart attack that year, and that after having typed my manuscript, she had changed the way in which she viewed death. She now believed that death was fated!

Now came the time to convince Jarod. I knew he had lined up a nine-week internship with an investment banking firm in Washington for the first part of the summer, so it stood to reason that he would want to come home and relax for the final six weeks of summer. The task ahead of me would be difficult, but I hoped not impossible. I would just have to convince him that the rewards of writing a book from the point of view of a middle-aged woman would outweigh the hardships. I had to let him know that it would challenge his creativity, but the reward would be that he wrote a book that would be a winner.

"Jarod, there are even more things to be gained--things which are intangible like motivation, hard work, perseverance and long-term goal setting." He seemed unmoved by my plea. But, I had held back an additional reward which I now sprung on him. "Jarod, I will make you a deal you can't refuse. I will not only match, but I will beat any hourly wage you could possibly make for a six-week period of time--that in addition to the privilege of working at home." My bargain struck, but not without a little reservation on his part. As his mother, I knew he would be up to the task.

To keep the information mill going as a source of inspiration for my son, I made a round of calls to all those closely involved in my story, telling them that the book had begun and it was vital that they should get in their last-minute thoughts.

I called my mother to ask her what her parents thought about psychic power. She was in a wonderful mood since she was in a committed relationship with a most delightful man. He treated her so much better than my father. After she told me about where she and her companion, Manny, had gone and what fun they were having, I launched into my question. "Mom, your mother was psychic. She had dreams that came true. Can you tell me more about her?"

My mother went on to say that her mother came from a very tiny village on the border between Russia and Poland on the Polish side called, "Lumsa Geberna." She didn't know if any of the other members of her family had psychic tendencies as well.

Manny, who was listening to her, said his father also came from that very same village. We agreed that she and Manny were fated to be together. Then, I asked what my grandfather had thought of all this. My mother answered that back in those days no one knew much about the subject. "Since my father didn't know what to make of it, he just thought my mother was bright."

I quickly replied, "Having dreams that come true isn't a sign of being bright; it's something from beyond. How could he think there's intelligence involved in seeing the future?" This intrigued me because I considered how much further my grandmother could have gone with her gift had she lived in today's times.

One night while visiting Janet, she suggested that we look through an Indian folklore book as a reference for the Indian vision. We pulled the book from her shelf and began skimming through it.

All of a sudden, Janet turned to me and said, "Look at this." She was pointing to a passage on Indian customs. "It says that there is a meaning behind how a feather is pointing."

"What does a feather pointing down mean?" I asked her.

"It says that a feather pointing downwards means that the one wearing the feather is coming in peace."

In my vision, when I walked across the empty field and saw Barry, his feather was pointing down, and then we were friends. He came in peace, just as his feather indicated.

It was now the beginning of September and time to leave for Las Vegas. I was beginning to feel at home there. A couple of days before we were scheduled to leave, Robert called to invite us to dinner at Pierro's Restaurant. He planned the dinner for 8 p.m. on our first Sunday in Las Vegas. We told him that we'd love to join him.

I couldn't wait for the dinner party. I kept thinking that something wonderful was going to happen at this dinner. The stage seemed set for fate to intervene and help me with my book project. Then again, I didn't want my expectations to get too high for fear that I would be let down.

Nevertheless, I dressed for success the night of Robert's dinner party. Chuck and I sat at the best table with Robert and his wife and four other couples who had flown in from different parts of the country. One of the women at the table showed an interest in my story because she had a best friend who was a psychiatrist and did past-life regressions on some of her patients. She was fascinated by the human brain and the mysterious ways in which it works. The woman said that the psychiatrist told her that people are just starting to learn about the brain's capabilities.

After the dinner, I pulled Robert aside. "Robert, I am writing a book about my experiences, and I want to ask you for permission to use your name in my book." Before he had a chance to reply, I hurriedly added that I was not saying one bad thing about him.

I told him that I was going to mention that I had a memory of him in another lifetime in which he was the shaman of my tribe. As we hugged goodbye, Robert's hand touched my head--just like in the vision.

"You can use my name as long as you promise to give me an autographed copy." Having permission to use his well-known name in my book made me feel absolutely incredible.

"Robert, you have always been wonderful." That evening, Robert essentially validated my story. By lending his name to my book, he is telling the world that knows me, and he doesn't think that there is anything wrong with me-- that I am not crazy.

Although nothing could match the first night, the rest of the trip was exciting, too. We went to parties and met many interesting people. I returned home with renewed vigor, and my need to find out what exactly happened to me was as strong as ever. As soon as I could, I called Temple University. Chuck and I decided to register for a course on psychic phenomena.

Mary Ann called and, after I told her the news about our trip, she said she had something to tell me. She had related my story to a psychiatrist, a Dr. Daz, who worked in the same hospital. The doctor had emigrated from India and was very familiar with my type of illness as well as psychic phenomena. He believed that the universe randomly selects people for this kind of experience. He told Mary Ann that while I was sick, I was disassociating. Mary Ann explained to me that this meant splitting off a group of mental processes from the main body of consciousness. Daz said that, according to Eastern philosophy, disassociation is a good thing because it allows people to cope with their pain. Mary Ann was surprised to hear this since she had studied Western philosophy, which dictates that disassociation is a sign of illness and an unhealthy thing to do.

I thanked Mary Ann for asking her colleague about my experience. "It's interesting that two psychologists have two different opinions on the same topic, which just goes to show how complex the topic of the mind really is."

Then, I told her that Chuck (the skeptical Mortal Man) and I signed up for a course on parapsychology called, "Mystical Musings." When Mary Ann asked me who

was teaching it, I told her about Barbara Stapleton, who had studied under the Edgar Cayce Foundation.

From the very first day of Musings, I was the star of the class. After telling my story, people in the class were amazed. The students said it was the most interesting story and the most relevant to the material we were learning. As it turned out, all of the topics we studied, including out-of-body experiences, reincarnation, meditation, and spirit guides, were things that I personally experienced. Even the rituals we examined, such as talking to spirits, doing body work, aligning the body, and meditating, were things I had done my whole life without ever learning them from someone else. They came to me naturally.

During one of our classes, some of the students were

asking our instructor about trying some past-life regressions. Barbara told the class that she didn't necessarily know if it was a good idea to go back to another lifetime. She explained that we are all born with a veil over us and that is the reason why we don't remember our past lives. At that point, I raised my hand. Agreeing with Barbara, I told the class that you don't know what you may find when you go back to a past life. I said that when I remembered a past life, I remembered an enemy, and I suffered as a result. I warned the class that by regressing, they're opening a can of worms in which they may be getting more than they bargained for.

Later in the course, Barbara told us that a friend of hers who was a psychic was scheduled to come in the following week to speak to the class about her experiences.

When Barbara announced this, I remembered that Michael's Back to School Night was also next week, but I couldn't remember the date. I knew that if I went, I might run into Barry and Myrna. In a way, I wanted to see them again to tell them that I was definitely writing a book. However, if it came to a choice between Back to School Night or this course, I would choose to go to the psychic's lecture.

As it turned out, Back to School Night was the night after the lecture, so I was able to attend both. The psychic talked about many of her experiences, and I discovered a lot of similarities between hers and my own. She said that she sees spirits and talks with them which was just like I had done in the case of my father. She could accurately read people by relaying information that just comes into her head which I felt I could do with my words. One thing she said amazed both Chuck and me. She said that many people who become psychic get very sick emotionally at the time the power is coming to them.

Thinking about Back to School Night, it was curious that the event was held on the 14th of October and that it was Michael's fourth year of high school. Although I ran the risk of seeing Barry and Myrna, I figured that it was possible that Barry, who is such a busy surgeon, would not have time to attend Back to School Night. I decided to gain some information by doing my words.

On Barry, I got the words "search" and "deploy." Looking up "deploy" in the dictionary, I found "to arrange, place, or move strategically or appropriately." On Myrna, I got "resigned" and "decline." "Resigned" is defined as "submissive or acquiescent." From all four of these words, I pretty much assumed that they were both going to be there.

From Barry's words, I believed that he was going to look for me while he was there because he wanted to make amends or peace with me. He probably felt bad that I was never able to tell him what I had wanted to tell him. After all, we lived in the same neighborhood, and I had been a patient of his, so I figured he thought there was no need for animosity.

Back to School Night started at 8. However, if you wanted to hear the principal speak, you were to show up at 7:30. I recalled that Myrna once told me that when she and Barry went anywhere, Barry was always late. If I got to the auditorium at 7:30 and saw that Barry arrived early, too, then I felt that would indicate that he was there partly to see me. After all, people usually mingled right after the lecture and before actually visiting the classrooms.

As Chuck and I walked into the school building, we noticed that a crowd had already gathered. We stopped to talk to a few people we knew before heading to the auditorium.    Then, as I made my way through the auditorium door, the first person I saw was Barry Kramer.

Barry faced the entrance doors at the rear of the room rather than sitting in the front where all the early arrivals sat.  It was as if he was watching each person as they entered.  Right away, I knew that Barry was searching and deploying.  Then, I noticed Myrna off to the side.  She was talking to a group of women.

When Chuck walked in, I whispered, "Barry's here." Then, I turned and noticed that Barry was walking towards me.  He never hesitated, but walked directly up to me and asked, "Are you still talking to me?"

I assured him that I was, and I told him I wanted to talk to him about something.  "Can you come over here in private?" I asked.  Barry followed me over to the wall, and Chuck came over, too.  "I have to tell you something.  I'm nervous about telling you this, but something happened to me after my surgery and I became psychic."  Then, I proceeded to inform him that experts and psychiatrists knew about this and that I was even writing a book about it.

"You're in the book," I said.  "I am not out to hurt you." Chuck went on to tell him that his role in the book was favorable at which time I shook my head to indicate that not all of it was positive.  I told him that I had two psychic dreams and that he was in the second one.  I continued with my story while he listened intently.

Chuck tried to change the subject by asking Barry how he was doing.  "Fine," Barry answered.  "I am doing a lot of reconstructive surgeries."

After a pause in the conversation, Chuck asked, "How are you managing without your partner?  It must be like a divorce."

Barry replied, "It's worse than a divorce."

Chuck turned to me. "Linda, tell Barry about the word you got." I told Barry that I got the word "archenemy" on him and his partner before there had been any sign that they were breaking up. Apparently, Barry didn't hear me or didn't understand what "getting a word" meant because he asked me to repeat myself. When I repeated "archenemy" to him, he looked shocked.

When we finished speaking, he said, "We'll have to go out to dinner sometime."

I looked directly into his eyes. "You don't have to say that to me. I would go out, but I don't need to force people to be with me."

As soon as I said it, I watched his soft eyes harden as he grew angry. He stared into me. "Didn't Myrna call you?" he asked.

"No."

"I thought she called you."

"No," I said again. Then, I asked him where Myrna was. He pointed her out to me. I excused myself in order to go talk to her.

As I was about to leave, Barry said, "Okay, Linda, I'll wait for a copy of the book." What I took that to mean was that I would have no problem giving him a copy of the book if it became successful, but if it didn't, I would not bother him.

As I started walking over to Myrna, I kept in mind the words "decline" and "resigned." She must have sensed that I was coming because she met me halfway. The first thing I said to her was, "Myrna, something happened to me that affected me greatly, and because of it, I became psychic. Now, I am in the process of writing a book about it."

She shot me a really weird look as if she didn't like what I was telling her. She started to open her mouth when all of a sudden the school bell rang, indicating that it was time to meet with the individual teachers in their classrooms.

She seemed relieved. "I'd better go now or Barry will never find his way to the first class."

As she turned to leave, I called out to her, "Barry will fill you in on the rest." She was resigned about the fact that Barry spoke to me but declined to say much herself. Myrna hurried away without commenting.

Chuck and I went from class to class and only caught a glimpse of the Kramers one more time. On our way home, I said to Chuck, "Do you know why I encountered Barry in the woods during my past life? We were probably both lost."

Before going to bed, I went down to the basement, turned on the radio, and started to dance myself into a trance. I re-created the scene with Barry in the auditorium. I always pay particular attention to the first thing a person says to me. Barry asked me, "Are you still talking to me?" These words seemed to be in keeping with his appearance at the edge of the woods with his down-turned feather in his headpiece, signifying he had come in peace. Had Barry shown up that night to make peace with me? I had to think it was true. I began to feel a little bit better about him.

After taking myself out of the trance, I decided to pull up a word on him to describe what he thought of me writing a book. The words I got were "sensational" and "circumspect." I knew what "sensational" meant, but I looked up "circumspect." It means "cautious, watchful, or wary." Both words applied. On the one hand, he thought the idea of me writing a book was a thrilling experience, but he was certainly anxious about his part in the story. I also believed that Barry and Myrna would be on the lookout for me in the future.

The next day I expected Janet to call, and I couldn't wait to tell her what happened the night before. After listening to the details, Janet said, "Linda, you're this tiny, little person and Barry and Myrna just don't know what to do with you." I told her they'd probably do what they always do--nothing.

Later, when I told Chuck about Janet's observation, he laughed and said, "That's okay, I don't know what to do with you either."

The next night, Chuck and I went to dinner with a couple with whom we had recently become acquainted. The woman's name was Barbara. She is a brilliant person, and so her opinions about my experiences really meant a lot to me. Barbara showed so much interest in my experiences that I decided to tell her that I was in the midst of writing a book. She encouraged me to do so, saying my story was really unusual.

When I expressed my fears about this project, she gave me some great advice. She said, "You're only afraid of something because it is unknown; once it's known, it's no longer frightening." I have found that this bit of advice holds so much truth. I have applied it both to the creation of this book and the rest of my life.

I realized that success means that you only experience different things when you go outside of your house. When you return, you go right back to your same life or to the sameness of life. Barbara was on the same wavelength. She said it was in this period of sameness that humans accomplish their growth. The process of changing and learning happens not when you are experiencing something different, but when you are back in the sameness of life where you can reflect and analyze what happened. You can't judge something new unless you have something to judge it against, something that you have already experienced.

Before we left the restaurant, Barbara told me that I had a right to develop as a person in any way I wanted. If other people didn't like the way I was developing, then that was their problem, not mine. I really enjoyed talking to Barbara because she is someone who really understands.

Chuck and I continued to attend Mystical Musings, and we both felt the course was a very positive step for me. For the first time, I was surrounded by people who were into psychic phenomena and, therefore, could share in my experiences. Basically, I felt less like a freak of nature and more like a normal human being.

In order to take full advantage of this course, I went up to the instructor many times after class to tell her about my experiences relevant to that day's topic. After a while, she encouraged me to go further into the topic. She suggested that I study with experts who could teach me how to do out-of-body experiences. Eventually, I decided against this route because I was concentrating on life in the business world as well as my family and friends. If I were to go too far, I risked losing the most important people in my life. Instead, I poured my energies into this book.

As a result of this course, I started to meditate and exercise more frequently, and I continued to talk to my spirit guides on a regular basis. I asked them for specific things and, little by little, the things I asked for would come my way. One time I asked my spirit guides for new friends. Later that week, while Chuck and I were in a restaurant, we ran into a couple we hadn't seen in sixteen years. Before we knew it, we started to see them socially again.

Another request was for help with my book. Chuck

started doing business with a woman who was best friends with a literary agent. Then, I received a wonderful offer of help from a woman Chuck had done a favor for some time ago. The woman offered to meet with us and give us advice about what to do with my story.

It was all too strange. I figured that if anyone could help explain what all of this was leading up to, the Old Lady could. I walked in and sat down next to her. Then, I hugged and kissed her and asked, "Should I be sharing this story? Will other people learn from my soul's journey?"

She said, "Yes."

"Why?" I still had difficulty grasping the notion that people might be interested in what I had to say.

"It's in your essence; it's in your destiny," she replied.

One night, I couldn't fall asleep because I was engrossed in a thought. I was thinking about how funny it is that my doing words on people is so commonplace in our household. Although I only tend to do them when someone challenges me, my ability has become a normal thing that my family and friends live with and don't even think about. Of course, anyone outside my close circle of friends would probably say to me, "Hey, Linda, try this word--CRAZY."

# Chapter 16

As Thanksgiving weekend approached, I decided that it would be a good time to do some words on Barry and Myrna. I based this decision on a theory of mine called, "My Thanksgiving Theory." Chuck and I have signed some of our biggest deals right after Thanksgiving weekend. I've observed that when very successful people get together with their families for the weekend, they often get bored. They cannot shut down, and they find their minds wandering back to their business and its problems.

I figured that if my theory was right, it was very possible that thoughts of Linda Gilman had crossed both Barry and Myrna's minds. It had only been a few weeks since we met at Back to School Night. Therefore, it was a good opportunity to pull more words.

I was surprised when I got three words on each of them. On Barry, I got "reclaimant," "reserved," and "resigned." From these words, I decided that they at least wanted to be on good terms with us. Then, I wrote all of these words down on a piece of paper, and at the bottom of the paper, I wrote: "I think that in the future they will try to be nice to us--if they should see us face-to-face in the neighborhood. I believe that they just want to be on decent terms." I dated the paper and slipped it into my note pad on psychic material.

The very next day, Chuck ran into Myrna Kramer at the local cleaners. Myrna, who was at the shopping center for other errands, followed Chuck as he walked into the shop. Chuck said that she was as friendly as could be. In fact, she gestured to give him a kiss, but Chuck told her not to because she might catch his cold. Then, she asked him how he got his cold, and he told her he had picked it up from a couple with whom we had gone to dinner recently. She asked if I had a cold, too. Chuck said I was fine. Next, she asked how the kids were doing and Chuck answered, "Terrific!" Chuck asked about her kids, and she said that they were fine.

Before they parted, Myrna said, "Please make sure to tell Linda I send my regards."

When Chuck came home, he told me that he had some interesting news. Describing the encounter to me, he said that he never would have known that anything had ever happened between us.

"Stay right there--don't move an inch!" I warned him. I grabbed hold of my note pad and showed him what I had written the night before about Barry and Myrna. He studied it carefully.

"This one is really good, Linda." This time I scored big time. It was rare that Chuck was that impressed with my words, but this time they really shook him up.

When Pam called the next day, I told her the whole story. I informed Pam that Myrna was finally starting to act smart for herself. She thought she could yo-yo me like Barry said she does to others. Little did she know, she was messing with a psychic, and I had powers she was unaware of.

Pam laughed. "Whatever she's thinking, she is definitely showing a healthy respect for you." I had to agree that this was true. Pam also added, "Linda, you don't even need a telephone."

With the New Year, I tried to turn over a new leaf, and I resolved to follow a more religious path. I decided to speak to two rabbis. The first rabbi was Pam's husband, Lew.

"Lew, what happened to me? You know my story very well. Tell me what happened." Lew said that he had developed his own theory. He feels that the universe has a higher intelligence in it and that people can be like radios. Furthermore, those people with the strongest receivers can pick up signals from this higher intelligence.

"As you were becoming psychic, Linda, your receiver strength increased, and you tuned in and picked up these signals. You were also emitting strong energy, and some people were drawn into this energy field while others were repelled by it." Then, he explained that Barry and Myrna were repelled by my energy field because it was too strong for them. Lew went on to assure me that it was perfectly okay because whoever was in my life was in it for a reason and whoever was not in my life was not. This is the essence of life.

The next rabbi I spoke with was Hasidic, which means that he is part of a Jewish sect that strictly adheres to the Eastern European Jewish traditions dating back to the 18th century. The Hasidim are influenced by the teachings of the Kabbalah, the book of Jewish mysticism. He believes in prayer, religious zeal, and joy. I asked him what he thought had happened to me.

He revealed that he believes in reincarnation. "As a teacher of the Kabbalah, I deal with the part of the Jewish religion concerned with psychic phenomena." Then, he offered his own explanation regarding my past-life memory.

He explained that a soul has life. "The soul has a life as does the body. The soul, however, is on a journey that takes many lives to complete whereas the body is limited to just one lifetime." This made sense to me. He went on to say that the world isn't working right--it is plagued by with diseases, violence, broken homes, murders, ethnic cleansing, etc.

"If the creator, for some reason, wanted to elevate the consciousness of the world, he would start by giving experiences to certain people who could spread the word and help to change our society. I feel that you are one of those chosen to do this." His words made me feel a heavy sense of responsibility. Would I be able to spread the word and help people?

That night, I couldn't get the words of the rabbi out of my mind. Was I chosen because my son is a writer? Was I chosen because my husband is an agent and knows powerful people? Was I chosen because I had the right kind of support from my family to have been able to survive all of this?

In the last stage of my past-life vision, I walked out onto the field, and I was the special one. Had my field suddenly become the whole world?

Now, I believed that my past-life vision was both a real memory from another lifetime as well as a precognitive vision. It happened while I was conscious and in a trance. I believe it is real because almost everything in it played out in this lifetime. I remembered the words of Carol Horn when she spoke to Chuck during a dinner they attended. "Can you imagine--someone actually has visions that come true?"

Even though I could never figure out why Barry, Myrna, and Robert were all in my vision, in time I accepted that they were there with me, and this made me wonder whether people actually know each other from previous lifetimes. And do karmic relationships, good and bad, travel together from life to life? Is this why some people grab your attention in life, while others don't?

At times, I thought the memory would have made much more sense if Barry was the medicine man since he was the doctor. Robert as the brave warrior who scalped people would fit better with his very first career as a hairdresser. On the other hand, Robert's importance to my tribe did make sense since in real life Robert was the C.E.O. of a billion dollar company. Could it be that his power and importance from another lifetime followed him into this lifetime? Also, it was true that Barry was still cutting people, although this time it was for their own good. Was Barry drawn to surgery so he could correct his mistakes because he was a warrior in a past lifetime? Barry does surgical hairplants. Could it be that Barry, plug by plug, was helping someone he once scalped?

Then, there was Linda Gilman. Did I do a good deed by pulling the arrow out of Barry's shoulder, even though he was the enemy? When the Shaman heard what I had done, he put his hands on me. Did this gesture mean that I was blessed? In this lifetime, did I do a good deed by breaking the legacy and providing a wonderful home for my husband and kids? Was my psychic gift actually a blessing for this good deed?

One time, my son Michael asked me, "Why is it that when people remember their past lives, they were always a king or a queen or someone famous?" I told him that I really didn't know. In my past lifetime, I was just a plain Indian warrior, but I did a good deed!

I wondered why the final part of my vision, the part about Barry and I being friends, did not play out. I recalled Back to School Night when Barry suggested that we all go out to dinner again, and I said, "No." In effect, I actually tampered with this part of the vision. I did not try to rekindle a friendship. Perhaps, this means that by knowing the future, one can alter it.

## Chapter 17

To this day, I still don't know what really happened when I felt the wave of energy pass through me during my nervous breakdown. Was it a spiritual integration? If so, was it responsible for my transformation from a shy, reclusive person into an extrovert who wants to share her story with the world?

I know that when I felt the pop in my heart, I suddenly experienced a new burst of energy. Had I not had that extra jolt, I truly feel that the trauma I was going through could have killed me. Was I supposed to live so that I could begin my special mission in life? Does everything happen for a reason? All I know for sure is that I couldn't just let my story fade away like some long-forgotten memory. I had to keep it alive and share it with the world. This book is how I chose to do it.

During the breakdown, I developed the ability to read people's minds by pulling up words. Where were these words coming from? I have a rather limited vocabulary. Not only were many of the words the kind I would never use, many of the words I had never even heard of. I'm accurate enough to know that they're coming from some new place in my brain. Still, I don't have all the answers.

Yet, one thing I learned from this ability to pull up words is that people's feelings are constantly changing. How someone feels about a particular topic one day may not necessarily be how that person feels the next day or the next week or the next month.

Just before I finished my manuscript, I asked the question, "What is happening to me?" I got the word "restitution," which is defined as "restoration to, return to, or recovery of a former position or condition." Does this mean that my breakdown was really a recovery--a chance to return to my potential? Because of the violence and abuse in my background, I had retreated to my cave like a wounded lion. After a long period of licking my wounds, I recovered my former strength. Now, I am ready to conquer the jungle.

Beginning with this book, I have occasionally been accused of trying to make the events in my life fit these psychic experiences. However, in my second dream, I was in a hospital. Never once did I go to a hospital during my nervous breakdown. If I wanted to make the dream fit, I easily could have gone to one. There were certainly times when I really needed to go to one, but I knew from the dream that I would save myself in the end. Rather than making things fit into my dream, I was trying to use my dream as a guide for doing the right thing.

In the last part of my past-life memory, Barry and I were friends. This was another part that I could have easily tried to make fit, but I didn't. When Myrna sent me the birthday card saying, "Hope we can get together soon," I didn't respond. When I saw Barry at Back to School Night and he suggested that we go out to dinner again, I said, "No." For these reasons, I deny the accusations that I tried to alter my life in an attempt to mimic my dreams and my vision. On the contrary, I altered my life by using the dreams and my vision as guides to help me to avoid negative consequences.

And then there is the part about me being the special one. What is so special about Linda Gilman? Maybe it's that Linda Gilman is a survivor. Maybe it's that Linda Gilman's spirits have protected her and now expect her to share with others what she learned through her catharsis. That would make her special.

At this point, Barry and Robert have faded from our lives. Chuck no longer does business with Robert, but we still see him at conventions, and we have a standing invitation to his home when we're in Los Angeles. We never see Barry anymore, except for a few times while Chuck was jogging down the road, Barry drove by and waved.

I did decide to ask a few more questions to see which words would come up on the Kramers. First, I asked how Barry and Myrna felt about what had happened between us. I got the word "incongruous." It is defined as "unsuitable, not harmonious." Then, I asked how they felt about my book. I got "enterprise," which is "an undertaking, especially a bold or difficult one." But, last of all, I needed to know what they finally thought of our offer. I pulled up, "existentialism," which is defined as " a philosophical theory emphasizing that man is responsible for his own actions and freely chooses his development and destiny." I believe that this is true, but I have to admit that those two people crossing my path certainly affected my destiny. After having had such an abnormal experience, I am now the happiest I have ever been, and I feel the most normal that I have ever felt. Becoming myself has been my greatest reward so far.

I'm still working to improve myself. As frightened as I am of getting up before a group of people to speak, I took a public speaking course this past fall. By making myself take this class, I conquered one of my worst fears. However, it wasn't easy. When my teacher invited the class to come up to present their first speech, I raised my hand.

"You'd better let me go right now or I think I will have a heart attack." I wasn't kidding. My heart raced faster and faster as I anticipated having to go up in front of all of those people.

I can't say that my delivery was the best, but the class always enjoyed hearing about my unusual experiences. I know that many students in the class did not believe in psychic phenomena, but my speeches held their attention. I think that they all related to my fears. Even if they did not experience my particular fears, my pain touched them. Maybe they remembered their own pain while hearing about mine.

Even Mary Ann began to see my side and believe in my visions. When I recently called Mary Ann, asking for her final diagnosis, she said, "You were able to transcend your psychic pain into an emotional triumph." When I asked her if she had changed her opinions about psychic phenomena, she replied, "I'm not so quick to doubt people anymore."

I sometimes have a hard time believing that a few years have passed since my catharsis. For one, the woodpeckers never returned. Every year they reappear on schedule and peck away at the trees, but they no longer attack the house. Although it seems bizarre, the disappearance of the woodpeckers has left an imprint on my mind. It will forever remind me of that turning point in my life.

Also, while I basically have the same personality, my behaviors are very different. Now I look forward to business trips because I am not as afraid to fly. This new-found confidence helps me to be much more outgoing. I talk to people so easily about my story. I feel good about being with virtually anyone because I have stopped dwelling on other people's opinions of me.

Carol has always maintained that no one knows what normal is and that by facing your painful memories, you are able to achieve mental health. Pam feels we're all born perfect apples but someone or something throws us against the wall and puts dents in our shiny exteriors.

Janet believes that we are all born perfect and good. She believes that, in life, the only things that are real that you take with you when you die are your good deeds and the spirit of your relationships. Janet is busy producing a children's program, so she can share her music, songs, and laughter with the next generation. Using her talents, Janet relates positive messages to young kids.

My mother is happy that we have become closer. Since my father died, she has developed into a wonderful role model. She's the happiest she's ever been in her life, and I've found that I now look up to her with the greatest of respect.

My sons have become stronger because of my courage to face my past. They are both proud of what Chuck and I have accomplished so far in this lifetime. The boys always remember the advice I gave them while they were growing up. I said, "Remember that out of over more than 100 million sperm, you were the sperm that hit the egg. You were the fastest swimmer. If you can do that, you have the potential to do almost anything."

Keeping that in mind, Jarod joined the family business where he can use his own abilities and talents to help bring the business to a new level. So, Jarod is on his way towards meeting his full potential. And, to reflect the fact that it is now a family business, we changed the name to Gilman Licensing Associates.

Mike's life has dramatically changed as he has adapted successfully to college life at George Washington University. Although he misses his family, he loves the new-found freedom. Despite the distractions of a co-ed dormitory and a grueling fraternity pledge schedule, Michael came through his first semester making the dean's list.

Chuck is looking forward to an even bigger year as we both prepare to fly to Atlanta for a convention. He is currently working on a deal with Supermodel and Actress Kathy Ireland and a company that would license her name for exercise equipment. We are both invited to a party in her honor in Atlanta, and many celebrities will be attending.

Chuck no longer works with Robert and his successful company, Skechers. Although Chuck has many new clients, he still refers to Robert and the people who used to work for L.A. Gear as "the Tribe."

Recently, Chuck and Michael came within inches of a potentially-fatal car accident while they were on a skiing trip. After they knew they were okay, Chuck looked up to the stars and thanked his spirit guides. This impressed me since only three years ago, he had a problem using the word, "psychic."

What is "psychic"? Is it the sixth sense? Psychic is unimaginable unless you've experienced something psychic yourself. I marvel at the number of people I speak to who, after listening to my story, come back with unusual tales of their own. Whether or not people believe me doesn't really matter much to me anymore. Many people have a hard time accepting the subject.

To me, psychic experience is just a part of my normal, everyday existence. Through dreams, I have seen the worst disasters of my life before they happened. Was my awareness of the Number Four actually a warning? Perhaps it was a foresight that eventually took me across a time line and into the Fourth Dimension. I believe that my glimpse into my past and future has broadened my awareness of life's bigger picture. Or, maybe my fate was about to be sealed, and it was Divine Intervention. Whatever the explanation, my visions altered the way I perceived many aspects of my life.

When I think about my father today, I finally can start to be objective. He went through a lot of trouble to find a way to earn my forgiveness. Now, I can remember wonderful things about him as well. It's a shame that we weren't able to work out our relationship while he was still alive, but maybe in death we were finally able to get it right. Wherever he now rests, I hope he knows that I did love him, and I hope he's at peace.

I called Pam to congratulate her on her recent promotion. It happened on a day when I was having a nasty flashback. I told her that until I met Chuck, nobody ever cared about what the emotional traumas did to me. Pam replied, "Obviously no one was concerned when you were a child or you wouldn't have had your nervous breakdown."

I thought I just had a thick physical scar left over from my childhood, and I wanted to fix it. However, by cutting into my physical scar, I learned that the silent ones underneath were the most painful ones. The trauma of a lifetime surged through my body. My Pandora's box opened, and my demons were released. I dealt with forgiveness and rejection, and I dealt with pain and hurt and anger. I was able to breathe more freely as I peeled the layers of sorrow from my being. I opened up spiritually, and, for the first time, I truly felt alive. I never knew that, inside us all, live silent scars.

# Epilogue

SILENT SCARS:
We all have them; we all give them.
Only love and understanding can heal them.

# About The Author

Linda Gilman is best described as passionate, spirited, kind, intelligent, funny, courageous and interesting. She has two sons, who love her very dearly and a wonderful marriage. Linda is an adviser to her husband in the family business and frequently travels around the country with him on business trips. Once a recluse, Linda now thoroughly enjoys meeting new people, both famous and not-so-famous, and revels at the chance to promote her book, "Silent Scars."

Linda would appreciate any comments you may have about her book and may be reached at the following e-mail address: SilentScar@aol.com.